8-5-76

Piers Plowman

MANCHESTER MEDIEVAL CLASSICS *General Editor* G. L. Brook

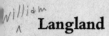

Langland

Piers Plowman

Selections from the B-text
as found in Bodleian MS. Laud Misc. 581

EDITED WITH AN INTRODUCTION
NOTES AND NEW PROSE TRANSLATION
by Stella Brook

MANCHESTER UNIVERSITY PRESS

BARNES & NOBLE BOOKS · NEW YORK

Published by MANCHESTER UNIVERSITY PRESS
Oxford Road, Manchester M13 9PL

UK ISBN 0 7190 0622 8

USA HARPER & ROW PUBLISHERS INC
BARNES & NOBLE IMPORT DIVISION

US ISBN 0 06 496091 4

Printed in Great Britain by T. & A. CONSTABLE LTD
Hopetoun Street, Edinburgh EH7 4NF

Contents

1924082

Acknowledgements

I should like to express my gratitude to all critics, translators and editors who have so greatly contributed to my own appreciation of the poem. Lack of specific reference does not imply lack of thanks.

Certain special acknowledgements are due: to Mrs Bernadette Philipsz, who with great patience and accuracy prepared the typescript of the text, which I have collated with photostats of the manuscript; to my husband, Professor G. L. Brook, who has helped and encouraged me at every stage and has given me all the benefits of his criticism; to the late Dr Florence E. Harmer, Reader in English Language and Literature at the University of Manchester, who first awakened me to the love of *Piers Plowman* and who, with much kindness and wisdom, fed my enthusiasm over many years; and to the Librarian and staff of the Bodleian Library for providing photostats of MS. Laud Misc. 581 and for allowing me to use them.

S. B.

August 1974

To my husband

The Ward Bequest

This volume is published with the aid of a grant from the Ward Bequest, a fund available to the University of Manchester for the publication of works of scholarship in History and English. This is the fifteenth volume published under the terms of the fund

Introduction

Piers Plowman, like many other medieval poems, confronts the reader with a series of question marks. No precise answer can be given to the obvious queries: who wrote it, and when? One can say, however, that it was written during the second half of the fourteenth century. Its first, tentative, form seems to have been composed in the mid-1360s; its revised, and greatly expanded, second version—at least in part—in the late 1370s; its final version in the late 1380s or the 1390s. All these presumptions have been mulled and argued over, but they still provide a rough guide to dating.

Who wrote *Piers Plowman*? Traditionally, a man called William Langland, of whom nothing certain is known, though a note to one of the many manuscripts of the poem suggests that he was the son of a certain Stacy de Rokayle. If occasional apparently autobiographical details in the poem can be taken at their face value, he would seem to have been a Clerk in minor Holy Orders (not a priest, since he refers to his wife and daughter). Various references within the poem make it clear that he was familiar with two parts of the country: London and Malvern. This double association with London and the West Midlands is borne out linguistically by verbal forms used in the poem. In the early years of the present century it was fashionable to argue that the three versions of the poem represent the work of several different poets. Mercifully, this suddenly intruded theory has made a quiet, gradual withdrawal and one can now, once again, speak of the three versions, known as the A, B and C texts, as the work of one man and refer to him by his traditional name of Langland. One can also, without entering into a long discussion of questions of authorship, use one of the three texts to cast light on another. The present volume of selections is taken from the B version, but, as can be seen from the Notes, the C-text is occasionally used to give a clearer meaning to details of translation.

Piers Plowman draws on a number of conventions and modes of its times. It is set in the framework of the dream or vision. Such a framework can be a mere tiresome formality; when handled skilfully, as Langland handles it, it permits the easy and convincing interplay between the 'marvellous' (in the etymological sense) and the everyday. The poem opens in the familiar medieval setting of a morning in May but the accepted, stylised enchantment of full springtime is here anchored firmly to the specific place, 'Malvern hills'. The personal association is infused into the traditional generality. In many ways, *Piers Plowman* reaches out to didactic and homiletic writings of its own and preceding centuries: in its Scriptural references and accepted interpretations of them, in its expositions of sins and virtues, with pungently apt illustrations. It also has links with works of straight or satirical social and political criticism, since it refers, often in biting terms, to certain contemporary events or ways of life. Above all, it is cast in the mode of an allegory, and the Middle Ages had an enormous taste for allegory.

Definitions of allegory are bewildering in their variety and their subtlety. Perhaps the simplest approach is to see allegory as a development of metaphor. A metaphor suddenly and briefly recognises a likeness between two apparently unconnected things; allegory works out the implications of that recognition. To say 'life is a pilgrimage' is a metaphor; to write *Pilgrim's Progress* is to develop the metaphor into allegory. The successful development depends on the possession of a particular kind of imaginative vision.

At any point in the history of literature a certain mode of writing can become fashionable and, consequently and regrettably, induce authors with no innate feeling for such a mode to try to express themselves in it. For example, not all Elizabethan and Jacobean dramatists who attempted the form of the blank verse play were well advised in their efforts. Similarly, many would-be medieval allegorists floundered hopelessly in a medium to which they were temperamentally unsuited. In this case, however, the results were even more unfortunate, since not merely a literary fashion was involved. Allegory is not just a style of writing, it is a way of looking at things, tangible and intangible. It certainly does not consist in the nominal personification of intangibles, in the mere prefacing of the names of abstractions with a capital letter; simply to call anger Anger, or truth Truth, is little more than a typographical device. For the genuine allegorist, anger and truth are as real as the man next door, and real in the same kind of way. Abstract and concrete, visible and invisible, palpable and impalpable, belong to one and the same world. Consequently, easily and without force, abstract qualities or ideas attach to themselves the behaviour and speech of concrete entities. But this is not the end of the story. The successful creation of allegory also involves what might be called a harmony of double vision. The 'concrete' behaviour of abstractions must not step out of line with their fundamental, definable, non-allegorical nature.

The surface narrative of the allegory must be in keeping with the implied moral or spiritual or intellectual statement that underlies it. The words and actions of Conscience personified, for instance, must be such that one can recognise in them the promptings of one's conscience in a given situation. The allegorist might be compared to a tight-rope walker. His balance is precarious. If he overbalances on one side, his personifications will become so completely humanised that their proper signification is lost sight of, and their actions and speech become grotesquely inappropriate to their nature. If he overbalances on the other side, he may make an impeccable abstract statement, but the story through which he intends to convey that statement totally fails to come alive. Many writers of Middle English allegory overbalance on one side or the other; Langland possessed a rare and assured steadiness of balance. Allegory was, for him, a natural medium.

So far, allegory has been used to refer to the writing of a creative work. When the term is used with reference to medieval writings, however, there is a complication, since it can also mean the 'allegorical interpretation' of a work, above all, of the Bible. The interplay between creative and interpretative allegory is complex and difficult to determine. However, without going into details of argument, it can be said that Langland does on occasion draw on traditional allegorical interpretations of the Bible and transmute them into elements in his own creative allegory. For instance, when, in the opening lines of Section D, Christ riding into Jerusalem on Palm Sunday is seen by the Dreamer as resembling not only Piers, but the Good Samaritan, there is a back reference to a preceding passage of the poem in which Langland makes use of a traditional biblical interpretation which sees the Good Samaritan of the parable as an 'allegory' of Christ. An even more striking example of the interplay between interpretative and creative allegory can be seen, also in Section D, in the argument between Truth, Mercy, Righteousness and Peace which is woven into the description of Christ's Harrowing of Hell. This argument has a long history. It has, as its root source, a verse in Psalm LXXXV (LXXXIV Vulgate): 'Mercy and truth are met together: righteousness and peace have kissed each other'. Even before Christian exegetical allegory seized on the possible developments of the verse, a Jewish *midrash* personified the four qualities, saw them as attributes of God and as involving a dilemma, which may be roughly stated thus: God's mercy, and His peace, may justify Him in creating man, but can His righteousness and truth justify such a creation? Subsequently, Christian exegesis transferred the dilemma to the question of God's redemption of man after Adam's fall from grace.

From this interpretative allegorical view of a verse from the Psalter, a whole creative allegory ramified, and became part and parcel of medieval thought. At its roots, it had the Latin versions of Hugh of St Victor and of St Bernard, but it rapidly grew into a vernacular tradition to be found, with various kinds and degrees of elaboration, across medieval Europe. There is nothing new or strange in Langland's introduction of the allegorical theme of the Four Daughters of God, as it has come to be called; there is however, a welcome freshness, a new vividness, in his presentation of a well-worn theme. Mercy, truth, righteousness and peace come alive in his imagination; in so many other works which draw on the same allegorical tradition they remain mere puppets, jerkily and arbitrarily manipulated.

It is easy to trace the development from allegorical interpretation to creative allegory when a single well-defined theme is in question. It is much less easy to say how far medieval creative allegory in general, and *Piers Plowman* in particular, is influenced by what might be called the fourfold *mystique* of patristic and medieval allegorical interpretation of the Bible (and of certain other texts). Once again, Christian interpretation did not appear out of the void; Philo Judaeus, writing from the point of view of one who wished to make some of the grosser details of the Old Testament more acceptable to the Greek Gentile mind, produced Jewish allegorical interpretation. However, from the Christian point of view, the founding fathers of the system of allegorical biblical interpretation were the two great Alexandrians: St Clement of Alexandria and his pupil Origen. From them, the theory and tradition spread west across Europe. The theory is that, on the one hand, one has the literal meaning of the sacred text; on the other hand, one has various spiritual meanings revealed through and by the words. These spiritual meanings may concern matters of general belief vital to all Christians; they may refer to the right disposition and conduct of the individual soul of man; they may refer to the eternal life and glory of Heaven, to which the Christian aspires. A well known medieval summary of the theory is based on the interpretation of the single word *Jerusalem*—literally, the Palestinian city; spiritually (a) the Church Militant on earth; (b) the individual soul; (c) the Church Triumphant in Heaven.

It is certainly possible to find occasions on which Langland's writing clearly draws on the tradition of multiple interpretation. In a passage already alluded to, immediately preceding the events described in Section D, the Dreamer meets three figures, each of whom carries various, simultaneous meanings. The first of these is, at one and the same time, Abraham, the expectation of the patriarchs of the Old Testament, and the personification of Faith; the second is Moses, the

Old Law, and Hope; the third is the Good Samaritan, Christ, and Charity. Quite apart from such a clear instance of multiple meaning, it must always be borne in mind that, on the many occasions when Langland quotes or alludes to biblical texts, the likelihood is that he has in mind not merely the naked text, but a complex made up of text and an accepted gloss upon it, deriving from the long tradition of multifold interpretation.

However, it is one thing to recognise that a specific reference to biblical texts must be seen in the light of a possible multiple meaning; it is quite another to argue that Langland and other writers of his time deliberately composed their works in such a fashion that the modern reader must apply the criteria of fourfold exegesis in order to understand them. Such a case has been persuasively presented by some recent critics, but its rigorous pursuance can make nonsense of the obvious literal meaning of the text, and any interpretation which does violence to that meaning cannot be accepted unquestioned. This is not a merely modern view. A similar idea was expressed seven centuries ago by a biblical commentator who compared the literal meaning of Scripture to the foundations of a building, and said that the spiritual interpretations are unacceptable if they destroy those foundations. It must also be remembered that the extent of Langland's scholarship is uncertain. In spite of all his references to the Bible and to various other Latin works, one does not sense in his poem anything resembling Chaucer's breadth of book-learning or the narrower, but deep, book-learning of Wyclif or Pecock. It is well to remember the caution once advised by R. W. Chambers against imputing to Langland the wide-ranging familiarity with learned works which is possible to the modern student of medieval writings, thanks to the existence of accessible printed editions.[1]

The possible alignment of *Piers Plowman* with the methods of Scriptural exegesis is only one form of interpretation that has attracted present-day critics. Other critics have turned to the poem for evidence which it may provide on points of historical and social interest, for references which it may contain to particular individuals of its times, for its possible autobiographical details which may throw light on the origins and life of its author. Yet others have related it to the sermon literature of its times, and others to the medieval formulation of three ways of life, active, contemplative and mixed. Taken together, these diversities of critical approach pay one of the most sincere tributes that can be given to a poem which itself includes sincerity among its most notable characteristics: that is, the recognition that here is something

---

[1] *'Piers Plowman': Man's Unconquerable Mind* (London, 1939), p. 104.

for everyone. The appeal of the poem is not just for those whose interests reach back to the past. *Piers Plowman* has a great deal to say to the modern reader interested only in modern times. However, it cannot be read exactly as if it were a twentieth-century poem. Unless one understands that, for Langland, *reason* is a faculty which makes moral as well as intellectual judgments, or—to take a very different example—unless one remembers the difference between the social structures of fourteenth-century and twentieth-century England, one's comprehension of the poem will be limited and spoiled. The historical sense and sympathy are necessary and must be brought to bear. Nevertheless, the more one reads *Piers Plowman*, the more one becomes conscious of its timelessness. This timelessness can be seen even in small points; for example, in Section B, the ingenuities described by Avarice concerning shady commercial and currency transactions have considerable unforeseen aptness for the present-day reader. It can be seen in the recognition, relevant to all ages, that 'charity', the full, deep love for one's fellow beings, has many manifestations. The courtesy and generosity of such love is not the particular property of a particular group. Langland shows how 'charity' can walk the world in rags or in a king's robes, how it cuts across the divisive barriers of social and ideological categories, making rich and poor one in honest intent. His sympathy is always most deeply with the poor, but he does not deny the goodness that can be manifested by the rich. The real division he makes is not between rich and poor, but between those who live 'truly' and those who live 'falsely'.

This distinction between truth and falsehood is fundamental to Langland's thought and the way in which he presents it poetically. At the extremes of allegorical personification, Truth is God and Falsehood is the Devil. This can be seen in Section A, where Holy Church explains to the Dreamer the vision he has had of the confused, milling world of men behaving in different ways and by different standards. Even without her instruction, the Dreamer has been shown already as feeling towards a discrimination between true and false living; for instance, 'true' hermits live a life of ascetic penitence within their cells, whilst 'false' hermits roam up and down the country. Holy Church's explanation adds an authoritative, divine dimension to the Dreamer's innate and unaided perceptions. 'True-living', for Langland, means that one carries out the obligations of one's calling, whatever that calling may be. Monk or minstrel, bishop or beggar, lord or labourer, each has his appointed ways and his appointed tasks, and behind and beyond the honest fulfilment of these tasks lies the ultimate approval and benediction of Truth who is God.

At the same time, 'true-living' is not, in itself, a passport to ultimate salvation. In a passage not included in the present volume Langland describes how Truth sends a Pardon to Piers. This Pardon is introduced shortly after the events described in Section B. In it the terms of God's mercy are clearly extended to all those who have lived truly and, as such, have some claim to likeness with Piers himself, but the point is that this *is* a Pardon. Even those who have, in their various ways, 'lived truly', cannot just claim Heaven as their right. They still need mercy and forgiveness. The point is clearly implied, and then it is not taken up again for a long time.

Piers's reception of the Pardon marks the end of the first stage of the poem. The formula of the Pardon is simple and clearcut, consisting of a quotation from the *Quicunque Vult*, popularly known as the Athanasian Creed: 'they that have done good shall go into life everlasting: and they that have done evil into everlasting fire'. A priest who is standing by pours scorn on the document, saying, in effect, that it is not a Pardon at all. Piers rips the pardon apart, and says that he is henceforth going to devote himself to the contemplative, rather than the active, life. The Dreamer then broods on what he has witnessed in his sleep. He ponders on what is meant by 'they that have done good'. In Langland's phrase, this appears as Do Well. In thinking about the nature of Do Well he arrives, by what Professor Coghill has described as 'a grammarian's trick',[1] at a view of a related progressive series of ways of life: the life of Do Well, the life of Do Better, the life of Do Best. For a long time, the poem is concerned with the Dreamer's attempts to find a definition of the three terms. His search might be summed up as an attempt to find an intellectually satisfying definition, conveyed through his allegorical encounters with mental faculties and with authoritative learning. He rebels, on the grounds of intellectual doubt, and strays off into the temptations of Fortune and the fundamental sins of the bodily state: the lust of the flesh, the lust of the eyes, and the pride of life. Ultimately, aided by the power of memory, he is recalled to his earlier ways. The part of the poem included here in Section C shows the results.

The Dreamer is still struggling towards a clear definition of the 'good', the 'better' and the 'best' ways of life, but there is here an important innovation. So far, in his search for enlightenment, his questions have been directed to intellectual virtues; now the moral virtue, patience, dominates his search. The Dreamer's decision to abandon Clergy (book-learning) and to accompany Patience on his travels, along with Conscience, has a far-reaching effect on the shaping

---

[1] 'The Pardon of Piers Plowman', *Proceedings of the British Academy* xxx (1944), p. 321.

of the total allegory of the poem. Langland at last faces a problem which was quietly abandoned many hundred lines previously.

The problem was this: if 'true-living' is a peak in man's moral and spiritual endeavour, and is truly in accordance with the will of God, who is Truth, what more is needed? In the early part of the poem, a sharp contradistinction was made between the 'true' and the 'false' livers—one white, one black. At the same time, the 'true' livers were shown to be in need of God's Pardon. Why? The answer is demonstrated with the Dreamer's encounter with Haukyn, *Activa Vita* (Section C).

At first sight, and by his own description of himself, Haukyn epitomises those whom the Dreamer first classified, at the start of the poem, as 'living truly'. In the course of the description of his 'coat of Christendom', which rapidly merges into Haukyn's own confession of his sins, it becomes apparent how far even those who 'live truly' fall short of perfection. It is no accident that the description of the sins which stain Haukyn's coat so closely resemble those mentioned much earlier by the Seven Deadly Sins themselves in their confessions (see Section B). Langland here picks up the dropped thread and weaves it into his total argument: even those who 'live truly' are grossly stained with sin and stand in need of God's mercy and forgiveness. The divine process of mercy and forgiveness and reconciliation is set forth in the description of the Passion and the Harrowing of Hell (Section D).

It would have been so easy to have stopped here, with the magnificent moment of triumph and redemption. Langland, however, is not concerned with the tidy, satisfying ending. He is concerned with the continuing problems of life on earth, Christ's victory notwithstanding. The exaltation continues for a little time, with the coming of the Holy Ghost and the endowing of Piers with the seeds and the means of cultivation of grace, but then the sad fact becomes apparent: Holy Church itself is corrupted and attacked by the forces of sin, and Conscience is left alone, crying desperately for Grace and for Piers the Ploughman, who can beat down pride. In this ending lies the great difference between two of the greatest English writers of religious allegory, Bunyan and Langland. For Bunyan the trumpets ultimately sound on the other side; Langland's Dreamer ends where he started, in the temporal world, still crying out for the means to salvation, for the right way to live.

However, if in one way the poem ends as it began, with a search, in another way it ends as it began, with an answer. When, in Section A, Holy Church explains to the Dreamer the full meaning of his vision of the field of the world, she moves subtly and gradually from an emphasis on the importance of truth to an emphasis on the importance of love and shows him the inextricable eternal interlinking of the two. In the latter part of Section D, when the Dreamer, as an old man, appeals to Nature to tell him what he must learn during his remaining days on earth, the answer is: 'Learn to love'. Experience has brought the Dreamer full circle. He has, so to speak, tested his weight on what first came to him as an authoritative pronouncement, and satisfied himself as to its rightness. All that lies between the initial teaching and his final convinced assent shows him struggling, with painful and often obstinate honesty, towards the true definition of the good life, of its improvement, and of its ultimate best form.

The long search is punctuated by the intermittent entrances of Piers himself. One cannot exactly call Piers the 'hero' of the poem, though he is its name figure. He is, in his successive appearances, a crystallisation and epitome of a particular kind of goodness. When he first bursts in on the attempts of the penitents to make their pilgrimage to 'Saint Truth', in Section B, he simply represents the summing up of the ideals of 'true-living' and of total commitment to God who is Truth which the penitents' lives have hitherto lacked, as their confessions show, and towards which they are fumblingly reaching out. Subsequently, his stature enlarges. In the references made to him in Section C, in the debate which arises at the end of the banquet given by Clergy, his authority is recognised by Clergy as superseding his own. In a passage which lies, in the full text, between Sections C and D, Piers is seen as the guardian and defender of the tree of charity, whose fruit represents mankind. In the opening lines of Section D, where the Dreamer has his vision of the first Palm Sunday, he sees Christ riding into Jerusalem dressed in the 'armour' of Piers—the 'armour' of human nature. The same image is caught up again later in Section D when, after the Passion and the Resurrection, the Dreamer has a new vision in which

> Pieres þe Plowman was paynted al blody,
> And come in with a crosse . . .
> . . . riȝte lyke in alle lymes to owre lorde Iesu.

He asks Conscience whether this is Jesus or Piers; Conscience replies that the arms are those of Piers, but that this is Christ. It is tempting to reduce this imagery to a clear-cut statement that Piers here represents the human nature of Christ, as opposed to His divine nature, but Langland seems to intend something subtler and less theologically precise. His image of Christ assuming the armour of Piers is a kind of reverse of St Paul's exhortation to Christians to 'put on the whole armour of God'. (The image of Christ's clothing Himself in humanity, which has certain affinities with Langland's image, is found explicitly in a Middle English lyric by William Herebert, addressed to the Blessed Virgin, 'My robe he haueth opon'. It is also implicitly hinted in the phraseology of some liturgical prayers.) Finally, again in Section D, Piers is once more seen as 'the ploughman', but now he is the ploughman who furrows the field of the world through the Evangelists and Doctors, and sows the seeds of virtue and establishes the Church.

Many attempts have been made to formulate neatly the exact allegorical signification of Piers and of his appearances and disappearances in the poem. Such attempts have their attraction, but they are perhaps too neat. It is easy, in one's admiration of Langland as a great allegorist, to forget that he is also a great poet. Piers most certainly is an important part of Langland's allegorical structure, but, in the end, he is probably best seen as a figure created by Langland's *poetic* imagination; convincing, compelling, but not precisely translatable into plain terms. When one is actually engaged in reading the poem, one simply accepts Piers without trouble or questioning; it is only when one puts the poem down and reflects on it that one begins to puzzle about him.

Indeed, quite apart from the particular question of the precise significance of Piers himself, the best way in to a sympathetic understanding of the whole poem is to allow oneself, initially, to respond to its sheer poetic qualities. When one suspends one's examination of the allegory, and judges *Piers Plowman* simply as poetry, perhaps its most impressive characteristic is its rich variety. It can rise to sublimity, as in the magnificent account of Christ's Harrowing of Hell (Section D); it can show a deep tenderness, unusual in contemporary writings, for details of Nature. For many Middle English writers, 'Nature' provides a charming, but stylised, setting: the well ordered, formal garden, the disorderly, but nevertheless formalised, 'wild' countryside, both of them seen under the enchantment of the perfect sunny air of spring. Alternatively, 'Nature' may provide the explanatory moralist with many useful examples. Langland uses the conventions of his times, but he also really looks at the natural creation; he has a concern for the 'wylde worme vnder weet erthe' (Section C). In a passage not included in this volume, he ponders deeply on the questions of how the magpie learns to build her nest, and how some birds have learned to hide their eggs away in marshes and moorlands, safe from human view. Langland's poetry can also be beautifully funny, as in the tumbling, rumbustious account of the wedding procession which accompanies Meed (Section A) or in some of the details in the confessions of the Seven Deadly Sins (Section B).

If one tries to single out one common characteristic which is apparent, and equally present, in all the varying moods and shades of the poetry, that characteristic is, perhaps, a gift for compression and pungency. For example, the biblical account of the Fall of man is summed up in the terse, racy line: 'Tho Adam and Eue eten apples vnrosted' (Section B); Christ in His majesty, confronting the powers of Hell, says, quite simply: 'loue is my drynke' (Section D); the Dreamer, bewildered, tired, plodding doggedly along the path of his search is 'wolleward and wete-shoed' (Section D)—a vividly compact phrase to conjure up coarse clothes and wet feet. Sometimes Langland's gift for compression leads him to an image which the Metaphysical poets might well have envied, as, for example, in his lovely, oblique reference to the Incarnation (Section A), with all its homely imagery, when he says that Love 'was so heuy of hym-self' that Heaven could not hold it 'Tyl it hadde of the erthe yeten [eaten] his fylle'.

Although there is so much in Langland's poetry which is timeless and universal, the exact form in which he wrote is no longer current, though its influence can sometimes be seen even now; for example, in some of the early poems of W. H. Auden. The original English poetic form, part of the common heritage shared by all the various Germanic tribes, was that of the 'alliterative long line', in which alliteration was not an ornament, but a fundamental part of the structure—as fundamental as the rhyme scheme is to a sonnet. This was non-stanzaic, non-rhyming verse; the unit was the line, itself composed of the subtle balancing of two half-lines within it. The rhythm was freer and suppler than that of strictly metrical verse; one could not beat time to it. It was, however, a definite pattern of rhythm, full of delicate but clear variations, resulting from the exact placing of stressed syllables, pointed and emphasised by alliteration, amid a varying number of unstressed syllables. In Old English poetry the patterning of stresses is so clearly marked that it is customary to speak of each individual half-line as an 'A-type', 'B-type', and so on. After the Norman Conquest, the alliterative long line seems to disappear, for a time, in the poetry which has survived. It reappeared in the fourteenth century, particularly in the north and west of England, in a freer and looser, but still recognisable, form. It is in this fourteenth-century style of the alliterative long line that *Piers Plowman* is cast.

One of the difficulties for the modern translator lies in the satisfactory rendering of some of the alliterating words. When alliteration is essential to composition, a special vocabulary tends to be formed, a vocabulary of alternatives with differing initial sounds. One cannot, for example, simply call a man a man; one may need, in order to fit the needs of the alliteration, to call him a *wye*. Many of these alliterative alternatives cannot be reproduced in modern English, unless one resorts to hopeless archaism. Consequently, a modern version of *Piers Plowman* may give an effect of repetitiveness which is certainly not present in the original. Also, although a fondness for alliteration persists not merely in English writing, but in English speech, the steady, emphatic alliteration of Langland's verse-line cannot now be systematically echoed without some feeling of deliberation and preciosity— qualities which, once again, are certainly not present in the original. The alliterative long line 'comes natural' to Langland, just as the allegorical manner of thought 'comes natural' to him.

Handled badly, the alliterative long line can be mechanically contrived and utterly wearisome. Handled well, it is full of possibilities. Its definite but free rhythm links it to easy speech rhythm. *Piers Plowman* is not merely a good poem to read silently; it is a good poem to read aloud. The fall of the stressed alliterative syllables gives it the formality necessary to bring it beyond a purely conversational manner, without introducing a strained and special manner of utterance. Also, the whole principle of alliteration can lend itself to a particular kind of poetic heightening of homely speech. Rhyme intrudes on the consciousness; well-used alliteration unobtrusively sharpens it. In particular, alliteration can serve the terseness which has already been mentioned as one of Langland's characteristics, as in such a phrase as 'chewen here charite' (Section A).

Quite apart from the mode of his thought and the manner of his poetry, another factor must be taken into account, namely, the kind of English which was at Langland's disposal. Compared with modern English, fourteenth-century English has certain disadvantages; it is not, for example, such a good medium for expressing closely argued logical thought. Its syntax is too untidy, by our standards. On the other hand, precisely because it is less well-regulated, it has possibilities which no longer exist, particularly the possibility of easy exchange between the colloquial and the literary. A poet can use, without any sense of discrepancy, the disjointed style of ordinary speech side by side with the highest utterances of poetic imagination. To do this now means to move between different levels; to do it in the fourteenth century meant to do it as a matter of course. Middle English is a less sophisticated tool than the English at our disposal, but it is a very good tool when used by a good craftsman. Langland was an excellent craftsman.

Prefatory Note

Piers Plowman is divided into sections of varying length, each of them headed *Passus*. These Passus might be compared to the chapters of a novel. In this volume of selections, Section A includes most of the Prologue and the whole of Passus I and II; Section B is taken entirely from Passus V, with omissions; Section C includes most of Passus XIII and parts of Passus XIV and XV; Section D comprises the whole of Passus XVIII and most of Passus XIX and XX. All these numberings are taken from the B-text of the poem. The headings given to the various sections in the translation have no counterpart in the original; they are inserted merely to give the reader some general idea of the main theme of each section.

There are a number of manuscripts of the B text. MS. Bodleian Laud Misc. 581 is a carefully written manuscript with very few obvious scribal errors. Many years ago W. W. Skeat chose it as the basis for his edition. Much more recently Professor J. A. W. Bennett has said that 'there is no reason to question Skeat's choice of the Laud MS. as the best single copy of that version extant'. Scholarly collation of the various manuscripts of the B-text continues, but, until a definitive edition is produced, it seems reasonable to follow well-founded tradition and to use the Laud MS. as the basis of a printed text. In this volume the spelling of the manuscript is, in general, preserved, but *ff* is replaced by *F* and the use of capital letters has been adapted to modern custom. The punctuation is editorial. Abbreviations used by the scribe have been expanded. Latin quotations are counted in the line-numbering when they begin at the same point as the English lines; when they are indented, they are not included in the countings.

Biblical material is closely woven into the text of *Piers Plowman*, both in the form of untranslated quotations from the Vulgate and in the form of close translation or summary allusion to it. It is difficult to decide which of the available biblical translations should be followed in rendering the Latin. The obvious choice is the Douai version, since this is directly based on the Vulgate, but the use of Douai would present certain problems. For example, the 'God is charity' of Douai fits less aptly into Langland's references to love, in Section A, than does the 'God is love' of the Authorised Version.

One does not want an excessively modernised translation. Langland's Latin biblical quotations stand out, and are meant to stand out, against the general flow of his vernacular composition, and this emphasis must by reflected in translation. At the same time, one wants ready intelligibility. The version normally used in this translation is the ecumenical Revised Standard Version: Common Bible (1973), referred to henceforth simply as The Common Bible. When its readings deviate markedly from those of the Vulgate, other translations are used and these are indicated in the Notes. Minor grammatical differences, such as a variation between a singular and a plural pronoun, are left unnoted. Langland sometimes employs a kind of shorthand in his biblical quotations (and occasionally in his non-biblical Latin quotations), giving the first few words only and leaving the reader to supply the remainder for himself. When necessary, to make the sense clear, the truncated quotations have been amplified in translation. Such amplifications are shown by the use of brackets.

Select Bibliography

Editions

W. W. Skeat: *The Vision of William concerning Piers the Plowman, in three parallel texts*, 2 vols. (Oxford, 1924). This is still the only complete available version of all three texts of the poem. The notes and glossary provide a great deal of valuable information and retain their importance, even though subsequent research has caused some of Skeat's views to be modified.

J. A. W. Bennett: *Langland, Piers Plowman: The Prologue and Passus I-VII of the B text as found in the Bodleian MS. Laud Misc.* 581 (Oxford, 1972). The most recent edition of the earlier part of the B-text. It contains very full notes, which include much background information.

Colin Wilcockson: *Selections from Piers Plowman* (London, 1965). A well chosen selection, intended for the novice, with plenty of good introductory comment and with admirable illustrations.

George Kane: *'Piers Plowman': The A Version. Will's Visions of Piers Plowman and Do-Well* (London, 1960). The authoritative scholarly edition of the A-text.

Elizabeth Salter and Derek Pearsall: *Piers Plowman* (London, 1967). A convenient volume of selections from the C-text, with introduction.

Translations

J. F. Goodridge: *Langland, Piers the Ploughman* (Penguin Books, Harmondsworth, 1959, 1966). A lively prose translation, with a useful introduction.

Critical works

R. W. Chambers: *'Piers Plowman:* A Comparative Study', in *Man's Unconquerable Mind* (London, 1939). An earlier general approach which retains its helpfulness.

John Lawlor: *Piers Plowman: An Essay in Criticism* (London, 1962). A close and informative study.

R. J. Blanch (ed.): *Style and symbolism in 'Piers Plowman': A Modern Critical Anthology* (Knoxville, Tennessee, 1969). A collection of previously published articles.

S. S. Hussey (ed.): *Piers Plowman: Critical Approaches* (London, 1969). A volume of previously unpublished essays.

Piers Plowman

A

In a somer seson whan soft was the sonne
I shope me in shroudes as I a shepe were,
In habite as an heremite vnholy of workes,
Went wyde in þis world wondres to here.
Ac on a May mornynge on Maluerne hulles   [5
Me byfel a ferly, of fairy me thouȝte;
I was wery forwandred and went me to reste
Vnder a brode banke bi a bornes side,
And as I lay and lened and loked in þe wateres
I slombred in a slepyng, it sweyued so merye.   [10
    Thanne gan I to meten a merueilouse sweuene,
That I was in a wildernesse, wist I neuer where.
As I bihelde into þe est, an hiegh to þe sonne,
I seigh a toure on a toft trielich ymaked;
A depe dale binethe, a dongeon þereinne   [15
With depe dyches and derke and dredful of sight.
A faire felde ful of folke fonde I there bytwene,
Of alle maner of men, þe mene and þe riche,
Worchyng and wandryng as þe worlde asketh.
Some putten hem to þe plow, pleyed ful selde,   [20
In settyng and in sowyng swonken ful harde,
And wonnen that wastours with glotonye destruyeth.
And some putten hem to pruyde, apparailed hem þere-after,
In contenaunce of clothyng comen disgised.
In prayers and in penance putten hem manye,   [25
Al for loue of owre Lorde lyueden ful streyte,
In hope forto haue heueneriche blisse;
As ancres and heremites that holden hem in here selles,
And coueiten nought in contre to kairen aboute,
For no likerous liflode her lykam to plese.   [30
    And somme chosen chaffare, they cheuen the bettere,
As it semeth to owre syȝt that suche men thryueth;
And somme murthes to make as mynstralles conneth,
And geten gold with here glee synneles, I leue.
Ac iapers and iangelers, Iudas chylderen,   [35
Feynen hem fantasies and foles hem maketh,
And han here witte at wille to worche ȝif þei sholde.
That Poule precheth of hem I nel nought preue it here;

---

20 putten: MS put

A: The World and its Ways

One summertime, when the sun shone warmly, I clad myself in garments such as a shepherd wears and, dressed like a hermit whose actions conflict with his vows, I travelled far and wide to learn of marvels. However, one morning in May, on the Malvern hills, the strangest adventure happened to me, seemingly by enchantment. I was worn out with journeying and lay down to rest at the foot of a broad river-bank, and as I lay there, reclining and watching the water, I dozed off to sleep because of the pleasant sound of it. Then I dreamed a wonderful dream of being in a wilderness—where, I had no idea. As I looked up eastwards towards the sun, I saw a beautifully built tower on top of a mound. Below, there was a plunging valley, and within it a castle-keep, surrounded by deep, dark ditches of terrifying appearance. Between the two I was aware of a sweet meadow crowded with all kinds of people, poor and rich, working and going hither and thither as life in the world requires.

Some set themselves to plough and rarely took their ease, labouring hard at planting and sowing and gathering what wastrels squander through gluttony. Some turned to pride and dressed themselves accordingly, coming along tricked out in a display of fine clothing. Many turned to prayers and penance and, entirely for the love of our Lord, led an austere life in the hope of achieving joy in the Kingdom of Heaven: anchorites and hermits, for example, who stay in their cells and have no desire to roam about the land or to give any pleasure to their bodies by lecherous living. Some chose to live by trading: they prosper the better, as such men appear to us to thrive. Some chose to provide entertainment, as minstrels know how to, and to make money by their music—blamelessly, to my mind. But as for jesters and tellers of idle tales, the sons of Judas, who invent far-fetched stories and behave like fools, yet have their wits about them and could work, if necessary, I will not now set out to prove that St Paul speaks with them in

Qui turpiloquium loquitur etc. is Luciferes hyne.

   Bidders and beggeres fast aboute ȝede,   [40
With her bely and her bagge of bred ful ycrammed;
Fayteden for here fode, fouȝten atte ale;
In glotonye, God it wote, gon hij to bedde,
And risen with ribaudye, tho roberdes knaues;
Slepe and sori sleuthe seweth hem eure.   [45

   Pilgrymes and palmers pliȝted hem togidere
To seke seynt Iames and seyntes in Rome.
Thei went forth in here wey with many wise tales,
And hadden leue to lye all here lyf after.
I seigh somme that seiden þei had ysouȝt seyntes;   [50
To eche a tale þat þei tolde here tonge was tempred to lye
More þan to sey soth, it semed bi here speche.

   Heremites on an heep, with hoked staues,
Wenten to Walsyngham, and here wenches after;
Grete lobyes and longe, that loth were to swynke,   [55
Clotheden hem in copis, to ben knowen fram othere,
And shopen hem heremites here ese to haue.

   I fonde þere freris, alle þe foure ordres,
Preched þe peple for profit of hemseluen,
Glosed þe gospel as hem good lyked,   [60
For coueitise of copis construed it as þei wolde.
Many of þis maistres freris mowe clothen hem at lykyng,
For here money and marchandise marchen togideres.
For sith charite haþ be chapman and chief to shryue lordes
Many ferlis han fallen in a fewe ȝeris.   [65
But holychirche and hij holde better togideres,
The moste myschief on molde is mountyng wel faste.

   Þere preched a pardonere as he a prest were,
Brouȝte forth a bulle with bishopes seles,
And seide þat hymself myȝte assoilen hem alle   [70
Of falshed of fastyng, of vowes ybroken.
Lewed men leued hym wel and lyked his wordes,
Comen vp knelyng to kissen his bulles;
He bonched hem with his breuet and blered here eyes,
And rauȝte with his ragman rynges and broches.   [75
Thus þey geuen here golde glotones to kepe,
And leueth such loseles þat lecherye haunten.
Were þe bischop yblissed and worth bothe his eres,
His seel shulde nouȝt be sent to deceyue þe peple.

---

³⁹ is Luciferes hyne *supplied*   ⁶⁷ myschief: MS mychief

mind, but 'whoever utters filth' is a servant of Lucifer.

Mendicants and beggars bustled about, belly and pouch stuffed full of bread. They got their food by false pretences and fought over their ale. God knows, these thieving vagabonds go to bed gluttons and get up profligates, forever dogged by sleep and wretched sloth. Pilgrims and palmers banded together to seek the shrines of St James of Compostella and of saints in Rome. They went on their way full of learned tales and were free to lie for the rest of their lives. I saw some who said that they had sought out the shrines of the saints, but, in every tale that they told, it seemed by their speech that their tongues were tuned to lying rather than to telling the truth. A crowd of hermits with crooked staffs went off to Walsingham, with their lights-of-love following them. They were great, tall, lubberly fellows with no liking for work, who dressed themselves in habits to distinguish them from other people, and pretended to be hermits in order to live a life of ease. I saw all the four Orders of friars there, preaching to the people for their own profit and glossing the Gospel as seemed good to them, construing it to suit themselves out of greed for fine cloaks. Many of these learned friars clothe themselves as they please, for their money and their trade go hand in hand. For since charity has turned huckster and become pre-eminently the confessor of the rich, many strange things have happened in the course of a few years. Unless Holy Church and the friars can live in greater harmony, the greatest of earthly misfortunes will gain rapidly increasing hold.

There was a Pardoner who preached as if he were a priest. He produced a papal Bull with bishops' seals attached and said that he himself had power to absolve them all from breaches of fasting and from broken vows. Ignorant people believed him entirely and were pleased by what he said. They came up and knelt to kiss his Bulls. He blinded their eyes by thrusting his letter of indulgence in their faces and gathered in rings and brooches by virtue of his parchment roll. So people hand over their money to maintain gluttons and put their faith in wastrels who practise lechery. If the bishop were a holy man and worth his keep, his seal would not be sent out to deceive the people. However, it is not by permission of the

Ac it is nauȝt by þe bischop þat þe boy precheth,   [80
For the parisch prest and þe pardonere parten þe siluer
That þe poraille of þe parisch sholde haue, ȝif þei nere.
  Persones and parisch prestes pleyned hem to þe bischop
Þat here parisshes were pore sith þe pestilence tyme,
To haue a lycence and a leue at London to dwelle,   [85
And syngen þere for symonye, for siluer is swete.
  Bischopes and bachelers, bothe maistres and doctours,
Þat han cure vnder Criste and crounyng in tokne
And signe þat þei sholden shryuen here paroschienes,
Prechen and prey for hem, and þe pore fede,   [90
Liggen in London in Lenten, an elles.
Somme seruen þe kyng and his siluer tellen,
In cheker and in chancerye chalengen his dettes
Of wardes and wardmotes, weyues and streyues.
  And some seruen as seruantz lordes and ladyes,   [95
And in stede of stuwardes sytten and demen.
Here messe and here matynes and many of here oures
Arn don vndeuoutlych; drede is at þe laste
Lest Crist in constorie acorse ful manye. . . . .

  Wiþ þat ran þere a route of ratones at ones,   [100
And smale mys myd hem mo þen a þousande,
And comen to a conseille for here comune profit;
For a cat of a courte cam whan hym lyked,
And ouerlepe hem lyȝtlich and lauȝte hem at his wille,
And pleyde wiþ hem perilouslych and possed hem aboute.   [105
'For doute of dyuerse dredes we dar nouȝte wel loke;
And ȝif we grucche of his gamen he wil greue vs alle,
Cracche vs, or clowe vs and in his cloches holde,
That vs lotheth þe lyf or he lete vs passe.
Myȝte we wiþ any witte his wille withstonde,   [110
We myȝte be lordes aloft and lyuen at owre ese.'
  A raton of renon, most renable of tonge,
Seide for a souereygne help to hymselue:
'I haue ysein segges', quod he, 'in þe cite of London
Beren biȝes ful briȝte abouten here nekkes,   [115
And some colers of crafty werk; vncoupled þei wenden
Boþe in wareine and in waste where hem leue lyketh;
And otherwhile þei aren elleswhere, as I here telle.
Were þere a belle on here beiȝ, bi Iesu, as me thynketh,

---

101 myd: MS with   105 possed hem aboute: hem *supplied*

bishop that the scoundrel preaches, for the parish priest and
the Pardoner share between them the money that would go
to the poor of the parish, if it were not for them.

Rectors and parish priests complained to the bishop that
their parishes had been poverty-stricken since the plague
years, and asked for licence and permission to live in London
and sell their services in the chantries there, for money is
enticing. Bishops and Bachelors of Arts, Masters or Doctors
of Divinity, who are charged, under Christ, with the care of
souls and wear the tonsure as a token and sign that they
should hear the confessions of their parishioners, preach to
them and pray for them, and feed the poor, reside in London
in Lent and out of Lent. Some serve the king by reckoning up
his money or by claiming, in the Exchequer or the Chancery,
what is owing to him from wardships and ward-meetings,
from property with no owner and from the estates left by
aliens. Some take service with lords and ladies and act as
judges in the manorial courts, in the place of stewards. Mass,
Mattins and many of their Offices are said without devotion.
It is to be feared that, on the Last Day, Christ, seated in His
consistory court, will place many of them under His curse.

At that, a swarm of rats, along with over a thousand little
mice, quickly scurried forward and held a council to promote
their common advantage; for a court cat came when it pleased
him, pouncing on them nimbly and catching them as he
wished, playing a dangerous game with them and jostling
them about. 'We hardly dare to peep out for fear of all sorts
of terrors, and if we complain about his games he will
torment us all, scratching us, or clawing us, and holding us in
his clutches, so that our life becomes a misery to us before he
lets us go. If we could use our ingenuity in some way to
frustrate his desires, we could be great lords and live at ease.'

A highly esteemed rat, with a most persuasive tongue,
suggested what seemed to him a sovereign remedy.

'In the city of London', he said, 'I have seen men wearing
bright necklaces around their necks, and some with skilfully
fashioned collars. They go about without leashes wherever
they like, in warrens and wastelands and, as I am told, in
other places at other times. By Christ! It seems to me that if
there were a bell on their collar, one could know where they

Men myȝte wite where þei went and awei renne!   [120
And riȝt so', quod þat ratoun, 'reson me sheweth
To bugge a belle of brasse or of briȝte syluer,
And knitten on a colere, for owre comune profit,
And hangen it vpon þe cattes hals, þanne here we mowen
Where he ritt or rest or renneth to playe.   [125
And ȝif him list for to laike, þenne loke we mowen,
And peren in his presence þer while hym plaie liketh,
And ȝif him wrattheth, be ywar and his weye shonye.'
    Alle þis route of ratones to þis reson þei assented.
Ac þo þe belle was ybouȝt and on þe beiȝe hanged,   [130
Þere ne was ratoun in all þe route, for alle þe rewme of Fraunce,
Þat dorst haue ybounden þe belle aboute þe cattis nekke,
Ne hangen it aboute þe cattes hals, al Engelonde to wynne;
And helden hem vnhardy and here conseille feble,
And leten here laboure lost and alle here longe studye.   [135
    A mous þat moche good couthe, as me thouȝte,
Stroke forth sternly and stode biforn hem alle,
And to þe route of ratones reherced þese wordes:
'Thouȝ we culled þe catte, ȝut sholde þer come another
To cracchy vs and al owre kynde, þouȝ we croupe
                                        vnder benches.   [140
Forþi I conseille alle þe comune to lat þe catte worthe,
And be we neuer so bolde þe belle hym to shewe;
For I herde my sire seyn, is seuene ȝere ypassed,
Þere þe catte is a kitoun þe courte is ful elyng.
Þat witnisseth holiwrite, whoso wil it rede: [145
    Ve terre vbi puer rex est, etc.
For may no renke þere rest haue for ratones bi nyȝte.
Þe while he caccheth conynges he coueiteth nouȝt owre caroyne,
But fet hym al with venesoun; defame we hym neuere.
For better is a litel losse þan a longe sorwe,
Þe mase amonge vs alle þouȝ we mysse a schrewe.   [150
For many mannus malt we mys wolde destruye,
And also ȝe route of ratones rende mennes clothes,
Nere þat cat of þat courte þat can ȝou ouerlepe;
For had ȝe rattes ȝowre wille ȝe couthe nouȝt reule ȝowreselue.
'I sey for me,' quod þe mous, 'I se so mykel after,   [155
Shal neuer þe cat ne þe kitoun bi my conseille be greued,
Ne carpyng of þis coler þat costed me neure.
And þouȝ it had coste me catel biknowen it I nolde,

¹³³ it *supplied*

were going, and run away. Just so', this rat continued, 'reason makes it clear to me that, for our common advantage, we should buy a bell of brass or shining silver, fasten it on a collar and hang it on the cat's neck, so that we can then hear whether he is chasing about, or resting, or running out to play. If he is in the mood for sport, then we can peep out and appear in his presence as long as his playful mood continues; but if he grows angry, then we can beware and avoid his path.'

The whole assembly of rats agreed to this plan, but, when the bell had been bought and hung on the collar, there was not one rat in the whole throng that dared fasten the bell round the cat's neck—not for the whole kingdom of France— nor hang it round the cat's throat—not to gain possession of all England! They admitted their timidity and the feebleness of their plan, and counted all their labour and their long deliberation as lost.

A mouse who, it seemed to me, showed much good sense, stepped forward resolutely and quickly and stood in front of them all, addressing these words to the assembly of rats:

'Even if we killed the cat, another one would come to scratch us and all our tribe, even though we crept under the benches. So my advice to all our people is to leave the cat alone and never be so foolhardy as to show him the bell, for, seven years since, I heard my father say that, where the cat is a kitten, the court is in a sorry state. Holy Scripture bears witness to this, if anyone chooses to read it: "Woe to you, O land, when your king is a child!" For no one can rest there at night on account of the rats. Let us not malign him; so long as he is catching rabbits he has no desire for our flesh, but feeds wholly on game. A little loss is better than a long sorrow and the confusion that would prevail among us all, even though we got rid of a tyrant. For we mice would destroy many a man's malt and you crowd of rats would tear people's clothes to pieces, if it were not for that cat of the court who knows how to pounce on you; for if you rats had your own way, you would not know how to rule yourselves. For my part,' said the mouse, 'I have sufficient foresight to say that neither the cat nor the kitten shall ever be crossed on my advice. Nor must there be any talk of this collar, which never cost me anything (though even if it had cost me money, I should refuse to agree to it), but let him do what he likes at his

C

But suffre as hymself wolde to do as hym liketh,
Coupled and vncoupled to cacche what thei mowe.   [160
Forþi vche a wise wiȝte I warne wite wel his owne.'
    What þis meteles bemeneth, ȝe men þat be merye
Deuine ȝe, for I ne dar, bi dere God in heuene! . . . .

What this montaigne bymeneth and þe merke dale
And þe felde ful of folke, I shal ȝow faire schewe.   [165
A loueli ladi of lere, in lynnen yclothed,
Come down fram a castel and called me faire,
And seide: 'Sone, slepestow? Sestow þis poeple,
How bisi þei ben abouten þe mase?
Þe moste partie of þis poeple þat passeth on þis erthe,   [170
Haue þei worschip in þis worlde, þei wilne no better;
Of other heuene þan here holde þei no tale.'
    I was aferd of her face, þeiȝ she faire were,
And seide: 'Mercy, madame, what is þis to mene?'
'Þe toure vp þe toft,' quod she, 'Treuthe is þereinne,   [175
And wolde þat ȝe wrouȝte as his worde techeth;
For he is fader of feith, fourmed ȝow alle
Bothe with fel and with face, and ȝaf ȝow fyue wittis
Forto worschip hym þerwith þe while þat ȝe ben here.
And þerfore he hyȝte þe erthe to help ȝow vchone   [180
Of wollen, of lynnen, of lyflode at nede,
In mesurable manere to make ȝow at ese;
And comaunded of his curteisye in comune þree þinges;
Arne none nedful but þo, and nempne hem I thinke,
And rekne hem bi resoun; reherce þow hem after.   [185
That one is vesture, from chele þe to saue,
And mete atte mele for myseise of þiselue,
And drynke whan þow dryest, ac do nouȝt out of resoun,
That þow worth þe werse whan þow worche shuldest.
For Loth in his lifdayes, for likyng of drynke   [190
Dede bi his douȝtres þat þe deuel lyked;
Delited hym in drynke, as þe deuel wolde,
And lecherye hym lauȝt, and lay bi hem boþe;
And al he witt it wyn þat wikkede dede:
    Inebriamus eum vino, dormiamusque cum eo
    Vt seruare possimus de patre nostro semen.
Thorw wyn and þorw women þere was Loth acombred   [195
And þere gat in glotonye gerlis þat were cherlis.
Forþi drede delitable drynke, and þow shalt do þe bettere;
Mesure is medcyne, þouȝ þow moche ȝerne.

pleasure. Let them catch what they can, whether they are on the leash or off the leash. My warning to every sensible person is to recognise his own interests.'

Let the carefree guess what this dream means for, by dear God in Heaven, I dare not!

Now I will tell you plainly the meaning of this mountain and the gloomy valley and the meadow thronged with people.

A beautiful lady, dressed in linen, came down from a castle and spoke kindly to me, saying: 'Are you asleep, my son? Do you see these people, so busily engaged in a turmoil of activity? If they achieve honour on earth, most of those living in this world wish for nothing better. They are not concerned with any heaven except the present.'

In spite of her beauty, her face filled me with awe. 'If you please, lady, what does this mean?' I asked.

She said: 'Truth lives within the tower on the hill, and He wishes you to do as His word teaches you. He is the Father of faith, who created you all in bodily shape and gave you five senses with which to worship Him during your time here. So He commanded the earth to provide you all with wool and linen and the necessary means of livelihood, to enable you to live in a reasonable measure of comfort. In His courtesy, He ordained that three things should be common to all, and these alone are necessary. I will count out their names in order and you must then repeat them. The first is clothing, to preserve you from cold; then food at meal-times, to relieve your discomfort; and drink, when you are thirsty—but observe moderation, lest you become the worse for drink when you ought to be working. The pleasures of drink caused Lot, in his time, to do the devil's pleasure in his behaviour towards his daughters. As the devil wished, he took his delight in drink, and lechery seized hold of him, and he lay with both of them. He put the blame for that evil deed wholly on wine, for his daughters said: "Come, let us make [our father] drink wine, and we will lie with him, that we may preserve offspring through our father." Lot then was overwhelmed through wine and through women and begot knavish sons in gluttony. So go in fear of the enjoyments of drink; thus, you will do better! Moderation is a good prescription, even though your craving is great. Not everything that your stomach demands

It is nauȝt al gode to þe goste þat þe gutte axeþ,
Ne liflode to þi likam þat leef is to þi soule.   [200
Leue not þi likam, for a lyer him techeth,
That is þe wrecched worlde wolde þe bitraye.
For þe fende and þi flesch folweth þe togidere,
This and þat sueth þi soule and seith it in þin herte;
And for þow sholdest ben ywar I wisse þe þe beste.'   [205
    'Madame, mercy', quod I, 'me liketh wel ȝowre wordes;
Ac þe moneye of þis molde, þat men so faste holdeth,
Telle me to whom, madame, þat tresore appendeth?'
    'Go to þe gospel', quod she, 'þat God seide hymseluen,
Tho þe poeple hym apposed wiþ a peny in þe temple,   [210
Whether þei shulde þerwith worschip þe kyng Sesar.
And God axed of hem of whome spake þe lettre,
And þe ymage ilyke þat þereinne stondeth.
"*Cesaris*", þei seide, "we sen hym wel vchone."
    "*Reddite Cesari*", quod God, "þat *Cesari* bifalleth,   [215
Et que sunt dei, deo, or elles ȝe done ille".
For riȝtful reson shulde rewle ȝow alle,
And kynde witte be wardeyne ȝowre welthe to kepe,
And tutour of ȝoure tresore, and take it ȝow at nede;
For housbonderye and hij holden togideres'.   [220
Þanne I frained hir faire for hym þat hir made:
'That dongeoun in þe dale þat dredful is of siȝte,
What may it be to mene, madame, I ȝow biseche?'
    'Þat is þe castel of care; whoso comeþ þerinne
May banne þat he borne was to body or to soule.   [225
Þereinne wonieth a wiȝte þat Wronge is yhote,
Fader of falshed, and founded it hymselue.
Adam and Eue he egged to ille,
Conseilled Caym to kullen his brother;
Iudas he iaped with Iuwen siluer,   [230
And sithen on an eller honged hym after.
He is letter of loue and lyeth hem alle;
That trusten on his tresor bitrayeth he sonnest.'
    Thanne had I wonder in my witt what womman it were
Þat such wise wordes of holy writ shewed,   [235
And asked hir on þe hieȝe name, ar heo þennes ȝeode,
What she were witterli þat wissed me so faire.
    'Holicherche I am', quod she, 'þow ouȝtest me to knowe,
I vnderfonge þe firste and þe feyth tauȝte,

<hr />

200 f. þat leef is to þi soule. Leue not þi likam *supplied*   204 sueth: MS seest

is good for your spirit, and not everything that is dear to your soul gives nourishment to your body. Put no trust in your body, for it is taught by a liar, namely the wicked world, which desires to betray you. The devil and the flesh combine to dog your footsteps. Both of them pursue your soul and make their voices heard in your heart. I am giving you this good advice so that you may be on your guard.'

'Thank you, lady,' I said. 'What you say pleases me well. But tell me: the wealth of this world, to which people cling so fast—to whom does that treasure belong?'

'Turn to the Gospel', she said, 'that God Himself proclaimed, when people put a question to Him in the temple about a coin, asking whether they should use it to honour Imperial Caesar. God asked them to whom the inscription referred and whose portrait was stamped on it. "Caesar's", they said. "We all see that clearly." "Render [therefore] to Caesar", said God, "the things that are Caesar's, and to God the things that are God's; otherwise you do amiss." For the just principles of reason ought to govern you all, and natural good sense ought to be the guardian of your money and the keeper of your treasure, handing it out to you when necessary, for these two are the allies of thrift.'

Then I asked her courteously, in the name of her Maker: 'If you please, lady, what is the meaning of that castle-keep in the valley, which is so fearful to behold?'

'That is the Castle of Sorrow. Whoever enters it may curse the fact that he was ever born. One whose name is Wrong dwells there. He is the begetter of falsehood and its founder. He incited Adam and Eve to sin and put it into Cain's heart to kill his brother. He tricked Judas with the Jews' money and afterwards hanged him on an elder-tree. He hinders the working of love and lies to all who put their trust in his treasure, promptly betraying them all.'

Then I was perplexed in my mind as to what manner of woman this might be, who expounded Holy Scripture with such wisdom, and conjured her by the high name of God to tell me truly, before she departed, who she was that gave me such good counsel.

'I am Holy Church,' she said. 'You ought to know me. I first received you and taught you the faith, and you gave me

And brouȝtest me borwes my biddyng to fulfille   [240
And to loue me lelly þe while þi lyf dureth'.
  Thanne I courbed on my knees and cryed hir of grace,
And preyed hir pitousely prey for my synnes,
And also kenne me kyndeli on Criste to bileue,
That I miȝte worchen his wille þat wrouȝte me to man: [245
'Teche me to no tresore, but telle me þis ilke,
How I may saue my soule, þat seynt art yholden'.
  'Whan alle tresores aren tried,' quod she, 'trewthe is þe best;
I do it on *deus caritas* to deme þe soþe;
It is as derworth a drewery as dere God hymseluen.   [250
  Whoso is trewe of his tonge and telleth none other,
And doth þe werkis þerwith and wilneth no man ille,
He is a god bi þe gospel agrounde and aloft,
And ylike to owre Lorde, bi seynte Lukes wordes.
Þe clerkes þat knoweþ þis shulde kenne it aboute,   [255
For cristene and vncristne clameþ it vchone.
  Kynges and kniȝtes shulde kepe it bi resoun,
Riden and rappe down in reumes aboute,
And taken *trangressores* and tyen hem faste,
Til treuthe had ytermyned her trespas to þe ende.   [260
And þat is þe professioun appertly þat appendeth for knyȝtes,
And nouȝt to fasten a Fryday in fyue score wynter;
But holden wiþ him and with hir þat wolden al treuthe,
And neuer leue hem for loue ne for lacchyng of syluer.
  For Dauid in his dayes dubbed kniȝtes,   [265
And did hem swere on here swerde to serue trewthe euere;
And whoso passed þat poynte was *apostata* in þe ordre.
  But Criste, kingene kynge, kniȝted ten,
Cherubyn and seraphin, suche seuene and anothre,
And ȝaf hem myȝte in his maieste, þe murger hem þouȝte;   [270
And ouer his mene meyne made hem archangeles,
Tauȝte hem bi þe Trinitee treuthe to knowe,
To be buxome at his biddyng; he bad hem nouȝte elles.
  Lucifer wiþ legiounes lerned it in heuene,
But for he brake buxumnesse his blisse gan he tyne,   [275
And fel fro þat felawship in a fendes liknes,
Into a depe derke helle, to dwelle þere for eure;
And mo þowsandes wiþ him þan man couthe noumbre
Lopen out wiþ Lucifer in lothelich forme,
For þei leueden vpon hym þat lyed in þis manere: [280

²⁴⁴ kenne: MS kende

your pledge [through your godparents] to carry out my bidding and love me faithfully for the whole of your life.'

Then I went down on my knees and implored her mercy, begging her piteously to pray for my sins and to teach me to believe in Christ with all my being, so that I might do the will of my Maker.

'You who are esteemed holy, do not teach me how to acquire treasure, but tell me this one thing: how can I save my soul?'

'When all treasures are put to the test,' she said, 'truth is the best. I appeal to the text "God [is] love" to prove this true. It is as precious a jewel as dear God Himself. The man who speaks the truth and nothing else and acts in accordance with it, wishing no one any ill, is, as St Luke tells us in the Gospel, a god on earth and on high, and resembles our Lord. Scholars who know this ought to spread this knowledge abroad, for all men, Christians and non-Christians, have a claim to it. Reason requires that kings and knights should uphold it, travelling the country striking down offenders and binding them fast until Truth finally passes judgment on their sins. This, clearly, is the proper calling of knights: not to fast on one single Friday in a hundred years, but to take the part of men and women whose whole desire is for truth and never abandon them, either for love or for gain. In his time, David dubbed knights and made them swear on their swords to serve Truth for ever. Anyone who transgressed against that condition was an apostate to the Order. But Christ, the King of kings, created ten Orders of knighthood: cherubim and seraphim, seven of like kind and one other. In His majesty He gave them power and increase of joy, making them archangels over His humbler retinue. He taught them to know truth through the Trinity. His only bidding was that they should be obedient to His command. Lucifer, along with his host, learned this in heaven, but he forfeited his bliss because he renounced obedience and, in devil's shape, fell from that companionship into the dark depths of hell, to remain there for ever; and innumerable thousands more, loathsome in form, plunged down with Lucifer, because they believed in him who told this lie: "I will sit [on the mount of assembly]

Ponam pedem in aquilone, et similis ero altissimo.
And alle þat hoped it miȝte be so, none heuene miȝte hem holde,
But fellen out in fendes liknesse nyne dayes togideres,
Til God of his goodnesse gan stable and stynte,
And garte þe heuene to stekye and stonden in quiete.

    Whan thise wikked went out, wonderwise þei fellen,   *[285*
Somme in eyre, somme in erthe and somme in helle depe;
Ac Lucifer lowest lith of hem alle;
For pryde þat he pult out his peyne hath none ende;
And alle þat worche with wronge wenden hij shulle
After her deth-day and dwell wiþ þat shrewe.   *[290*
Ac þo þat worche wel as holiwritt telleth, .
And enden, as I ere seide, in treuthe, þat is þe best,
Mowe be siker þat her soule shal wende to heuene,
Þer treuthe is in Trinitee and troneth hem alle.
Forþi I sey as I seide ere, bi siȝte of þise textis,   *[295*
Whan alle tresores arne ytried treuthe is þe beste.
Lereth it þis lewde men, for lettred men it knowen,
Þat treuthe is tresore, þe triest on erþe.'

    'ȝet haue I no kynde knowing,' quod I, 'ȝet mote ȝe kenne me
                                      better,
By what craft in my corps it comseth and where.'   *[300*
    'Þow doted daffe,' quod she, 'dulle arne þi wittes;
To litel Latyn þow lernedest, lede, in þi ȝouthe;
    Heu michi, quod sterilem duxi vitam iuuenilem!
    It is a kynde knowyng', quod he, 'þat kenneth in þine herte
For to louye þi Lorde leuer þan þiselue;
No dedly synne to do, dey þouȝ þow sholdest: *[305*
This I trowe be treuthe; who can teche þe better,
Loke þow suffre hym to sey, and sithen lere it after.
For thus witnesseth his worde, worche þow þereafter;
For trewthe telleþ þat loue is triacle of heuene;
May no synne be on him sene þat vseth þat spise,   *[310*
And alle his werkes he wrouȝte with loue, as him liste;
And lered it Moises for þe leuest þing and moste like to heuene,
And also þe plente of pees moste precious of vertues.
    For heuene myȝte nouȝte holden it, it was so heuy of hymself,
Tyl it hadde of þe erthe yeten his fylle,   *[315*
    And whan it haued of þis folde flesshe and blode taken,
Was neuere leef vpon lynde liȝter þerafter,
And portatyf and persant as þe poynt of a nedle,

---

[302] *quod:* MS *quia*   [308] worche: MS worcheth

in the far north; [I will ascend above the heights of the clouds,]
I will make myself like the Most High." Heaven could not
retain those who trusted that this might be so. Transformed
into devils, they fell for a full nine days until God, in His
goodness, brought them to rest and pause and made heaven
close and stand still. When these evil ones went forth they fell
in strange fashion, some into the air, some into the earth,
some into the depths of hell; but Lucifer lies deepest down of
them all. Because of the pride that he displayed, his torment
is endless. All those who do evil will go and dwell with that
Evil One after they die; but, as Holy Scripture tells us, those
who do good and end their lives, as I have said, in Truth,
which is the best of all things, may be sure that their souls will
go to heaven, where Truth has its home in the Trinity and will
enthrone them all. So I say, as I said before, on the evidence of
these texts, when all treasures have been put to the test,
Truth is the best. Teach the ignorant (for the learned know it)
that Truth is the finest treasure on earth!'

'But I have no natural understanding of this,' I said. 'You
will have to teach me more clearly by which, and from which,
of my bodily skills it springs.'

'You silly, dim-witted fool!' she said. 'You learned too
little Latin when you were young: "Woe is me, for I led a
barren life in my youth!" There is an instinctive knowledge
in your heart which prompts you to love your Lord better
than yourself and to commit no deadly sin, even at the cost of
your life. This, to my mind, is Truth. If anyone can give you
better teaching, let him speak, and then digest what you have
heard. For this is the witness borne by God's word; act in
accordance with it!

'Truth tells us that Love is heaven's medicine, and no sin
can be found in the man who avails himself of that precious
remedy. It pleased God to perform all His works through
Love. He taught Moses that it was the dearest of all things
and the closest to heaven, the most precious of virtues and
also the abundant source of peace. It was so heavy in itself
that heaven could not hold it until it had eaten its fill of earth.
When it had taken on mortal flesh and blood, it was lighter
than the leaf on a lime-tree and as quick-moving and piercing
as a needle's point, so that neither armour nor high walls

That my3te non armure it lette, ne none hei3 walles.

Forþi is loue leder of þe Lordes folke of heuene,   [320
And a mene, as þe maire is bitwene þe kyng and þe comune;
Ri3t so is loue a ledere and þe lawe shapeth,
Vpon man for his mysdedes þe merciment he taxeth.
And for to knowe it kyndely, it comseth bi myght,
And in þe herte, þere is þe heuede and þe hei3 welle;   [325
For in kynde knowynge in herte þere a my3te bigynneth,
And þat falleth to þe fader þat formed vs alle,
Loked on vs with loue and lete his sone deye
Mekely for owre mysdedes to amende vs alle;
And 3et wolde he hem no woo þat wrou3te hym þat peyne,   [330
But mekelich with mouthe mercy he bisou3te
To haue pite of þat poeple þat peyned hym to deth.

Here my3tow see ensamples in hymselue one,
That he was mi3tful and meke and mercy gan graunte
To hem þat hongen him an hei3 and his herte þirled.   [335

Forthi I rede 3ow riche, haueth reuthe of þe pouere;
Thou3 3e be my3tful to mote, beth meke in 3owre werkes.
For the same mesures þat 3e mete, amys other elles,
3e shullen ben weyen þerwyth whan 3e wende hennes;
    Eadem mensura qua mensi fueritis, remecietur vobis.

For þou3 3e be trewe of 3owre tonge and trewliche wynne,   [340
And as chaste as a childe þat in cherche wepeth,
But if 3e louen lelliche and lene þe poure,
Such good as God 3ow sent godelich parteth,
3e ne haue na more meryte in masse ne in houres,
Þan Malkyn of hire maydenhode, þat no man desireth.   [345

For Iames þe gentil iugged in his bokes,
That faith withoute þe faite is ri3te no þinge worthi,
And as ded as a dore-tre, but 3if þe dedes folwe;
    Fides sine operibus mortua est, &c.

Forthi chastite withoute charite worth cheyned in helle;
It is as lewed as a laumpe þat no li3te is inne.   [350

Many chapeleynes arne chaste, ac charite is awey;
Aren no men auarousere than hij whan þei ben auaunced;
Vnkynde to her kyn and to alle cristene,
Chewen here charite and chiden after more.
Such chastite wiþouten charite worth cheyned in helle!   [355

Many curatoures kepen hem clene of here bodies,
Thei ben acombred wiþ coueitise, þei konne nou3t don it fram hem,

343 good: MS goed

could keep it out. So Love is the commander of the subjects of the Lord of heaven, and acts as an intermediary, just as a mayor does between the king and the common people. In the same way, Love is a leader and a lawmaker, assessing the fine which a man owes for his sins. To know it fully and intimately begins with a power which has its source and deep fount in the heart. For from instinctive knowledge within the heart there issues a power which belongs to the Father who made us all, who gazed on us with love and let His Son die humbly for our sins, to heal us all. He wished no evil to those who caused Him such suffering, but prayed in gentleness for mercy and pity on those who tortured Him to death. Here, in Himself alone, you can find examples showing that He was full of power, but gentle, granting mercy to those who hanged Him aloft and pierced His heart. Consequently I advise those of you who are rich to have pity on the poor. Although you have the power to summon them to the law-courts, be gentle in your dealings, for by the same standards that you measure with, falsely or otherwise, you yourselves will be weighed when you depart from this world: "the measure you give will be the measure you get".

'Even though you are truthful in your speech and earn your living honestly, and are as chaste as a child that cries when it is baptised, unless you truly love and give to the poor, liberally sharing the goods that God has sent you, you derive no more merit from Mass or other church services than Malkyn has from her virginity, when no one desires her. For St James laid it down in his Epistle that faith without action is worthless, and, unless it is succeeded by deeds, as dead as a doornail: "Faith apart from works is dead". So chastity without love shall be fettered in hell; it is as useless as a lamp without a light in it. Many chaplains are chaste, but love is lacking in them. No one is more avaricious than they are when they obtain preferment. They are without natural kindness towards their relations and towards all Christian people. They devour what they ought to give away in charity and clamour for more. Such loveless chastity will be fettered in hell! Many parish priests keep their bodies undefiled, but they are weighed down by covetousness and cannot put it from them, because

So harde hath auarice yhasped hem togideres.
And þat is no treuthe of þe Trinite, but treccherye of helle,
And lernyng to lewde men þe latter for to dele.   [360
   Forþi þis wordes ben wryten in þe gospel,
Date et dabitur vobis, for I dele ȝow alle.
And þat is þe lokke of loue and lateth oute my grace,
To conforte þe careful acombred wiþ synne.
   Loue is leche of lyf and nexte owre Lorde selue,   [365
And also þe graith gate þat goth into heuene;
Forþi I sey as I seide ere by þe textis,
Whan alle tresores ben ytryed, treuthe is þe beste.
Now haue I tolde þe what treuthe is, þat no tresore is bettere,
I may no lenger lenge þe with, now loke þe owre Lorde!'   [370

Yet I courbed on my knees and cryed hir of grace,
And seide: 'Mercy, madame, for Marie loue of heuene,
That bar þat blisful barne þat bouȝte vs on þe rode,
Kenne me bi somme crafte to knowe þe fals.'
   'Loke vppon þi left half, and lo, where he standeth,   [375
Bothe Fals and Fauel and here feres manye!'
   I loked on my left half, as þe lady me taughte,
And was war of a womman wortheli yclothed,
Purfiled with pelure, þe fynest vpon erthe,
Ycrounede with a corone, þe kyng hath non better.   [380
Fetislich hir fyngres were fretted with golde wyre,
And þereon red rubyes as red as any glede,
And diamantz of derrest pris and double manere safferes,
Orientales and ewages, enuenymes to destroye.
Hire robe was ful riche, of red scarlet engreyned,   [385
With ribanes of red golde and of riche stones;
Hire arraye me rauysshed, suche ricchesse saw I neuere;
I had wondre what she was and whas wyf she were.
   'What is þis womman', quod I, 'so worthily atired?'
'That is Mede þe mayde,' quod she, 'hath noyed me ful oft,   [390
And ylakked my lemman þat Lewte is hoten,
And bilowen hire to lordes þat lawes han to kepe.
In þe popis paleys she is pryue as myself,
But sothenesse wolde nouȝt so, for she is a bastarde.
For Fals was hire fader, þat hath a fykel tonge,   [395
And neuere sothe seide sithen he come to erthe.
And Mede is manered after hym, riȝte as kynde axeth;
      Qualis pater, talis filius: bona arbor bonum fructum facit.

397 bona: MS bonus

avarice has fastened them to it so firmly. Here is no Truth of the Trinity, but hell's treachery, teaching the laity to give less readily. On this account, these words are written in the Gospel: "Give, and it will be given to you"; for I hand out to you all! That is the key which turns the lock of love and releases my grace, to bring comfort to those who are sorrowful and burdened with sin.

'Love is life's healer, nearest to our Lord Himself, and also the straight path leading to heaven. So I say as I said before, by appeal to the texts, when all treasures have been put to the proof, Truth is the best. Now that I have told you what Truth is—an unsurpassable treasure—I can stay with you no longer. Our Lord keep you!'

Once again I went down on my knees and besought her mercy, saying: 'If you please, lady, for the love of Mary, our heavenly queen, who bore the blessed child that redeemed us on the cross, give me the skill to recognise Falsehood.'

'Look to your left! There stands Falsehood, and Flattery as well, and many of their companions.'

I looked to my left, as the lady told me, and perceived a woman dressed in splendid clothes trimmed with the finest possible fur. She was crowned with a coronet not surpassed even by the king's. Her fingers were handsomely adorned with rings of gold filigree set with rubies as red as glowing coals, with diamonds of the first water and with two kinds of sapphires, amethysts and aquamarines, as antidotes against poison. Her dress was costly, made of cloth dyed scarlet, ornamented with red-gold ribbons and precious stones. Her attire dazzled me; I had never seen such splendour. I was puzzled to know who she was and whose wife she might be.

'Who is this magnificently dressed woman?' I asked.

'That', she said, 'is the Lady Meed, who has often done me harm and slandered one whom I love, named Good Faith, telling lies about her to the authorities who are charged with the enforcement of the law. She is as much at home in the Pope's palace as I am myself, but this is not as truth would have it, for she is a bastard. Her father was Falseness, who is treacherous in his speech and never spoke a true word in his life. Meed takes after him, in accordance with the laws of nature: "Such as the father is, such is the son"; "every sound tree bears good fruit [but the bad tree bears evil fruit].'

I auȝte ben herre þan she, I cam of a better.
   Mi fader þe grete God is and grounde of alle graces,
O God withoute gynnynge, and I his gode douȝter,   [400
And hath ȝoue me Mercy to marye with myself;
And what man be merciful and lelly me loue,
Shal be my lorde, and I his leef, in þe heiȝe heuene.
   And what man taketh Mede, myne hed dar I legge,
That he shal lese for hir loue a lappe of *caritatis*.   [405
How construeth Dauid þe kynge of men þat taketh Mede,
And men of þis molde þat meynteneth treuthe,
And how ȝe shal saue ȝowself, þe sauter bereth witnesse:
      Domine, quis habitabit in tabernaculo tuo, &c.
And now worth þis Mede ymaried al to a mansed schrewe,
To one Fals Fikel-tonge, a fendes biȝete;   [410
Fauel þorw his faire speche hath þis folke enchaunted,
And al is Lyeres ledyng þat she is þus ywedded.
   Tomorwe worth ymade þe maydenes bruydale,
And þere miȝte þow wite, if þow wolt, which þei ben alle
That longeth to þat lordeship, þe lasse and þe more.   [415
Knowe hem þere, if þow canst, and kepe þi tonge,
And lakke hem nouȝt, but lat hem worth til Lewte be iustice,
And haue powere to punyschen hem; þanne put forth þi resoun.
   Now I bikenne þe Criste,' quod she, 'and his clene moder,
And lat no conscience acombre þe for coueitise of Mede.'   [420
   Thus left me þat lady liggyng aslepe,
And how Mede was ymaried in meteles me þouȝte;
Þat alle þe riche retenauns þat regneth with þe false
Were boden to þe bridale on bothe two sydes,
Of alle maner of men, þe mene and þe riche.   [425
To marie þis maydene was many man assembled,
As of kniȝtes and of clerkis and other comune poeple,
As sysours and sompnours, shireues and here clerkes,
Bedelles and bailliues and brokoures of chaffare,
Forgoeres and vitaillers and vokates of þe Arches;   [430
I can nouȝt rekene þe route þat ran aboute Mede.
   Ac Symonye and Cyuile and sisoures of courtes
Were moste pryue with Mede of any men, me þouȝte.
Ac Fauel was þe first þat fette hire out of boure,
And as a brokour brouȝte hir to be with Fals enioigned.   [435
Whan Symonye and Cyuile seiȝ here beire wille,
Thei assented for siluer to sei as bothe wolde.

429 chaffare: MS chaffre

I ought to rank more highly than she does, for I came of a better stock. My father is Almighty God, source of all grace, one God, eternal and uncreated, and I am his good daughter. He has given me Mercy as a dowry, and anyone who is merciful and loves me faithfully shall be my lord, and I will be his love, in heaven above. I will stake my life that any man who embraces Meed shall, for love of her, lose his share of real love. The Psalter shows how King David defines men who accept Meed and men who uphold truth and the way to achieve salvation, saying: "O Lord, who shall sojourn in thy tent? [Who shall dwell on thy holy hill? He who walks blamelessly, and does what is right, and speaks truth from his heart]."

'Meed is now about to be married to Falsehood-the-Fickle-Tongued, a wretched, accursed son of the devil. Flattery has cast a spell on the people with his beguiling speech and she is making this marriage at Liar's instigation. Tomorrow will be the lady's wedding day. If you are so minded, you can then find out who they all are, lowly or great, that hold that allegiance. Recognise them there if you can, but hold your tongue and do not censure them. Let them be until Good Faith comes to judgment and has the power to punish them; then state your case. Now', she said, 'I commend you to Christ and to His pure mother and never let the desire for Meed cause your conscience to trouble you.'

So the lady left me lying asleep and, in a dream, I saw how Meed was married. It seemed to me that all the fine retinue that participate in the rule of falsehood were invited to the wedding by both parties. Many people from all walks of life, poor and rich, were gathered to assist in the lady's marriage: knights, clergy, commoners, jurors, summoners, sheriffs and their clerks, tipstaffs and bailiffs, commercial brokers, purveyors and victuallers, advocates from the Court of Arches—I cannot count the host that swarmed around Meed. However, it seemed to me that Simony and Civil Law and jurymen were on the closest terms of all with Meed. Yet Flattery took the lead in fetching her from her chamber and, in the capacity of a matchmaker, brought her to be joined to Falsehood. When Simony and Civil Law saw what both parties desired they agreed, in return for payment, to say whatever the two wished.

Thanne lepe Lyer forth, and seide, 'Lo! here a chartre
That Gyle with his gret othes gaf hem togidere',
And preide Cyuile to se and Symonye to rede it.   [440
Thanne Symonye and Cyuile stonden forth bothe,
And vnfoldeth þe feffement þat Fals hath ymaked,
And þus bigynneth þes gomes to greden ful hei3:
   'Sciant presentes et futuri, &c.
Witeth and witnesseth, þat wonieth vpon þis erthe,
Þat Mede is y-maried more for here goodis,   [445
Þan for ani vertue or fairenesse or any free kynde.
Falsenesse is faine of hire for he wote hire riche;
And Fauel with his fikel speche feffeth bi þis chartre
To be prynces in pryde and pouerte to dispise,
To bakbite and to bosten and bere fals witnesse,   [450
To scorne and to scolde and sclaundere to make,
Vnboxome and bolde to breke þe ten hestes;
And þe erldome of enuye and wratthe togideres,
With þe chastelet of chest and chateryng-oute-of-resoun,
Þe counte of coueitise and alle þe costes aboute,   [455
That is, vsure and auarice; alle I hem graunte,
In bargaines and in brokages with all þe borghe of theft;
   And al þe lordeship of lecherye in lenthe and in brede,
As in werkes and in wordes and waitynges with eies,
And in wedes and in wisshynges and with ydel thou3tes,   [460
There as wille wolde and werkmanship failleth.'
   Glotonye he gaf hem eke and grete othes togydere,
And alday to drynke at dyuerse tauernes,
And there to iangle and to iape and iugge here euenecristene,
And in fastyng-dayes to frete ar ful tyme were.   [465
And þanne to sitten and soupen til slepe hem assaille,
And breden as burgh-swyn and bedden hem esily,
Tyl sleuth and slepe slyken his sides;
And þanne wanhope to awake hym so with no wille to amende,
For he leueth be lost; þis is here last ende.   [470
   And þei to haue and to holde, and here eyres after,
A dwellyng with þe deuel and dampned be for eure,
Wiþ al þe purtenaunces of purgatorie into þe pyne of helle.
3eldyng for þis þinge, at one 3eres ende,
Here soules to Sathan, to suffre with hym peynes,   [475
And with him to wonye with wo whil God is in heuene.

---

457 borghe: MS borgthe   461 werkmanship: MS wermanship
467 breden: MS bredun

Then Liar bustled forward, saying: 'Look! Here is a deed of gift which Guile, the great oath-swearer, has given them jointly.' He asked Civil Law to look it over and Simony to read it. Then Simony and Civil Law both stepped forward and spread out the deed drawn up by Falsehood. They began to proclaim in loud voices:

' "Let those present and those to come know, etc." All dwellers on earth, take note and witness that Meed is married for the sake of her possessions rather than for the sake of any virtue or beauty or gentle birth. Falsehood desires her because he knows her to be rich. Deceitful-tongued Flattery endows them by this deed, with the right to live like princes in pride and to despise the poor, to backbite, to boast, to bear false witness, to be scornful, to scold and to utter slanders, to be disobedient and to break the Ten Commandments boldly.

'I grant them in full the combined earldom of Envy and Wrath, with the castle of Strife and Immoderate-Idle-Chatter, the county of Covetousness and all the lands round about it, namely, Usury and Avarice in their bargainings and business dealings, together with the entire borough of Theft; in addition, the length and breadth of the whole lord's domain of Lechery, to wit, in deeds and words and wanton glances, in clothes and longings and in vain musings when desire remains and performance fails.'

He also gave them Gluttony and its accompaniment, Great Oaths, and the right to drink all day long in various taverns, gossiping there and joking and criticising their fellow Christians, and to eat on fast days before the proper time, then to sit at supper till sleep comes upon them, to breed like town-pigs and lie down on soft beds till sloth and sleep make their sides grow sleek; then to be awakened by Despair, lacking the will to amend their lives because they believe themselves to be lost. This is their final end.

And they and their heirs after them are to have and to hold a dwelling-place with the devil and be eternally damned, with all the appurtenances of Purgatory, into the pain of hell, yielding in return, at the end of a year, their souls to Satan, to suffer torments with him and dwell in sorrow with him as long as God is in heaven.

D

In witnesse of which þing Wronge was þe first,
And Pieres þe pardonere of Paulynes doctrine,
Bette þe bedel of Bokynghamshire,
Rainalde þe reue of Rotland sokene,   [480
Munde þe mellere and many moo other.
'In þe date of þe deuel þis dede I assele,
Bi siȝte of sire Symonye and Cyuyles leue.'

Þenne tened hym Theologye whan he þis tale herde,
And seide to Cyuile: 'Now sorwe mot þow haue,   [485
Such weddynges to worche to wratthe with Treuthe;
And ar þis weddyng be wrouȝte, wo þe bityde!

For Mede is moylere of Amendes engendred,
And God graunteth to gyf Mede to Treuthe,
And þow hast gyuen hire to a gyloure; now God gyf þe sorwe! [490
Thi tixt telleth þe nouȝt so, Treuthe wote þe sothe,
For *dignus est operarius* his hyre to haue,
And þow hast fest hire to Fals; fy on þi lawe!
For al by lesynges þow lyuest, and lecherouse werkes,
Symonye and þiself schenden holicherche,   [495
Þe notaries and ȝee noyeth þe peple.

Ȝe shul abiggen it bothe, bi God þat me made!
Wel ȝe witen, wernardes, but if ȝowre witte faille,
That Fals is faithlees and fikel in his werkes,
And was a bastarde ybore, of Belsabubbes kynne.   [500
And Mede is moylere, a mayden of gode,
And myȝte kisse þe kynge for cosyn, an she wolde.

Forþi worcheth bi wisdome and bi witt also,
And ledeth hire to Londoun þere lawe is yshewed,
If any lawe wil loke þei ligge togederes.   [505
And þouȝ Iustices iugge hir to be ioigned with Fals,
Ȝet beth war of weddyng, for witty is Truthe,
And Conscience is of his conseille and knoweth ȝow vchone;
And if he fynde ȝow in defaute and with þe fals holde,
It shal bisitte ȝowre soules ful soure atte laste!'   [510

Hereto assenteth Cyuile, ac Symonye ne wolde,
Tyl he had siluer for his seruise, and also þe notaries.

Thanne fette Fauel forth floreynes ynowe,
And bad Gyle to gyue golde al aboute,
And namelich to þe notaries þat hem none ne faille,   [515
And feffe False-witnes with floreines ynowe;
'For he may Mede amaistrye and maken at my wille.'

---

486 weddynges: MS wendynges   488 engendred: MS engendreth

The first witness to this deed was Wrong, then Piers the Pardoner of the Pauline school, Bartholomew the Buckinghamshire under-bailiff, Reynold the steward of the district of Rutland, Mund the miller and many more besides: 'I set my seal to this deed in the year of the devil's dating, in the presence of Simony, and by permission of Civil Law.'

Theology was angry when he heard this talk and said to Civil Law: 'A plague on you for contriving such weddings to enrage Truth! May you regret it before this marriage is performed! For Meed is a true-born lady, the daughter of Compensation. God consents to the giving of Meed to Honest Labour, but you, God damn you! have given her to a trickster. Truth knows the true facts; this is not what the text tells you to do, for "the labourer deserves his wages", but you have tied her to Falsehood—shame on your law! You live wholly by lies and deeds of lechery. You and Simony bring disgrace on Holy Church. The notaries and the pair of you do harm to the people; by God! you shall both pay the penalty! You liars, you are well aware, unless you have taken leave of your senses, that Falsehood is faithless and treacherous in his acts and was born a bastard of the stock of Beelzebub, but Meed is a true-born lady of rank who might, if she chose, kiss the king as her cousin. So act wisely and sensibly and take her to London where the law is expounded, to see whether any law will permit them to share a bed. But even if the judges rule that she should be united with Falsehood, still be wary about the marriage, for Truth is wise and Conscience, who knows you all, is one of his council. If he finds you at fault, and siding with Falsehood, it will have heavy and bitter results for your souls in the end.'

Civil Law gave his assent to this, but Simony, and the notaries, too, refused, until he was paid for his services. Then Flattery produced a good pile of florins and told Guile to hand out money all round, especially to the notaries, 'so that none of them will fail us', and to give False Witness a large fee as a retainer, 'for he can bring Meed under control and bend her to my will'.

Tho þis golde was gyue grete was þe þonkynge
To Fals and to Fauel for her faire ʒiftes,
And comen to conforte fram care þe Fals,   [520
And seiden, 'Certis, sire, cesse shal we neuere
Til Mede be þi wedded wyf þorw wittis of vs alle.
For we haue Mede amaistried with owre mery speche,
That she graunteth to gon with a gode wille
To Londoun, to loke ʒif þat þe lawe wolde   [525
Iugge ʒow ioyntly in ioye for euere.'
     Thanne was Falsenesse fayne and Fauel as blithe,
And leten sompne alle segges in schires aboute,
And bad hem alle be bown, beggeres and othere,
To wenden wyth hem to Westmynstre to witnesse þis dede.   [530
     Ac þanne cared þei for caplus to kairen hem þider,
And Fauel fette forth þanne folus ynowe;
And sette Mede vpon a schyreue shodde al newe,
And Fals sat on a sisoure þat softlich trotted,
And Fauel on a flaterere fetislich atired.   [535
     Tho haued notaries none; annoyed þei were,
For Symonye and Cyuile shulde on hire fete gange.
     Ac þanne swore Symonye and Cyuile bothe,
That sompnoures shulde be sadled and serue hem vchone:
'And lat apparaille þis prouisoures in palfreis wyse;   [540
Sire Symonye hymseluen shal sitte vpon here bakkes.
     Denes and suddenes drawe ʒow togideres,
Erchdekenes and officiales and alle ʒowre regystreres,
Lat sadel hem with siluer, owre synne to suffre,
As auoutrie and deuorses and derne vsurye,   [545
To bere bischopes aboute abrode in visytynge.
     Paulynes pryues, for pleyntes in þe consistorie,
Shul serue myself, þat Cyuile is nempned;
And cartesadel þe comissarie, owre carte shal he lede,
And fecchen vs vytailes at *fornicatores*.   [550
     And maketh of Lyer a longe carte to lede alle þese othere,
As freres and faitours þat on here fete rennen.'
And thus Fals and Fauel fareth forth togideres,
And Mede in þe myddes and alle þise men after.
I haue no tome to telle þe taille þat hem folweth,   [555
Of many maner man þat on þis molde libbeth;
Ac Gyle was forgoer and gyed hem alle.
     Sothenesse seiʒ hym wel and seide but a litel,

---

535 flaterere: MS flatere   545 deuorses: MS deuoses

When the money was distributed, the recipients heaped thanks on Falsehood and Flattery for their rich gifts and came to soothe away Falsehood's troubles, saying:

'Rest assured, sir, we shall not desist until, by the exercise of our combined wits, Meed becomes your wedded wife. By our ingratiating words, we have so directed Meed's thoughts that she gladly agrees to go to London to see whether the law will give the verdict that you shall live together happily for evermore.'

Then Falsehood rejoiced and Flattery was similarly light at heart. They had everyone in the neighbouring counties summoned and told them all, beggars and the rest, to be ready to go with them to Westminster to witness this deed. Their next concern was about horses to carry them there, and Flattery produced a number of foals. He set Meed upon a newly shod sheriff; Falsehood rode a gently trotting juryman and Flattery a toady in splendid trappings. The notaries were aggrieved because they were left unprovided for and Simony and Civil Law would have to go on foot. However, Simony and Civil Law both swore that summoners should be saddled to serve them all:

'Have these Pope's nominees harnessed as palfreys! Simony himself will ride on their backs. Assemble the deans, sub-deans, archdeacons, bishops' delegates and all your registrars! Have them saddled with silver, to make them tolerate our sins, such as adultery and divorces and secret usury, so that they may carry bishops about when they go on their visitations. Confidential friends among the Paulines shall serve me, Civil Law, in pleading in the Consistory Court. Harness the bishop's officer! He shall draw our cart and get food for us from fornicators. And make Liar serve as a long cart to draw all the others who are on foot, such as friars and impostors!'

So Falsehood and Flattery set out together with Meed between them and all these others bringing up the rear. I have no time to describe the rag, tag and bobtail of all descriptions that followed them, but Guile headed and guided them all.

True Judgment took good note of him. He said little, but

And priked his palfrey and passed hem alle,
And come to þe kynges courte and Conscience it tolde,   [560
And Conscience to þe kynge carped it after.
'Now by Cryst,' quod þe kynge, 'and I cacche my3te
Fals or Fauel or any of his feres,
I wolde be wroke of þo wrecches þat worcheth so ille,
And don hem hange by þe hals and alle þat hem meynteneth!   [565
Shal neure man of molde meynprise þe leste,
But ri3te as þe lawe wil loke late falle on hem alle.'
And comanded a constable þat come atte furst,
To 'attache þo tyrauntz, for eny thynge, I hote,
And fettereth fast Falsenesse, for enykynnes 3iftes,   [570
And gurdeth of Gyles hed and lat hym go no furthere.
And 3if 3e lacche Lyer, late hym nou3t ascapen
Er he be put on þe pilorye, for eny preyere, I hote;
And bryngeth Mede to me maugre hem alle.'
        Drede atte dore stode and þe dome herde,   [575
And how the kynge comaunded constables and seriantz
Falsenesse and his felawschip to fettren an to bynden.
Þanne Drede went wi3tliche and warned þe Fals,
And bad hym flee for fere and his felawes alle.
    Falsenesse for fere þanne flei3 to þe freres,   [580
And Gyle doþ hym to go agast for to dye.
Ac marchantz mette with hym and made hym abide,
And bishetten hym in here shope to shewen here ware,
And apparailled hym as a prentice þe poeple to serue.
    Li3tliche Lyer lepe awey þanne,   [585
Lorkynge thorw lanes, to-lugged of manye.
He was nawhere welcome for his manye tales,
Oueral yhowted and yhote trusse;
Tyl pardoneres haued pite and pulled hym into house.
They wesshen hym and wyped and wonden hym in cloutes,   [590
And sente hym with seles on Sondayes to cherches,
And gaf pardoun for pens poundmel aboute.
Thanne loured leches, and lettres þei sent,
Þat he sholde wonye with hem, wateres to loke.
Spiceres spoke with hym to spien here ware,   [595
For he couth of here craft and knewe many gommes.
Ac mynstralles and messageres mette with hym ones,
And helden hym an half-3ere and elleuene dayes.
        Freres with faire speche fetten hym þennes,

597 mynstralles: MS mynstalles

he spurred his horse on and passed them all. He arrived at the
king's court and informed Conscience of the matter, and
Conscience then told the king.

'By Christ!' said the king. 'If I could lay hands on Falsehood,
or on Flattery, or an any of his companions, I would be
avenged on these wretched malefactors, and all their sup-
porters, and have them hanged by the neck! No one is to
bail out even the minor offenders; but let the judgment of the
law fall on all of them!'

He gave orders to an officer of the law, who promptly
appeared:

'Arrest these oppressors of the people at all costs, at my
command! Bind Falsehood fast, no matter what bribes are
offered! Strike off Guile's head; let him go no further! If you
seize hold of Liar, do not let him escape before he is put in
the pillory, whatever pleas are made; and bring Meed to me
in spite of them all!'

Dread, standing near the door, heard this ruling and the
king's order to officers and sergeants-at-law to shackle and
bind Falsehood and his company. Then Dread hurried off to
give warning to Falsehood and to bid him and all his com-
panions take to flight for fear.

Then Falsehood in his fright fled to the friars and Guile
took to his heels in terror of his life, but merchants encountered
him and made him stay with them. They shut him up in their
shop, dressed as an apprentice, to display their goods and
serve their customers. Liar went racing off light-footed. He
slunk about the alley-ways, tugged hither and thither by
many people, welcomed nowhere, despite all his tales, jeered
at everywhere and told to take himself off, until the Pardoners
took pity on him and hauled him into their house. They
washed and dried him and dressed him in rags, then sent him
to the churches on Sundays, equipped with seal-bearing
indulgences, distributing Pardons by the poundsworth all
round, in exchange for money. Then the doctors were
displeased, and sent letters asking him to live with them and
examine urine samples. Grocers asked him to inspect their
goods, for he was acquainted with their trade and knew of
many aromatic gums. However, on one occasion minstrels
and messengers encountered him and held on to him for six
months and eleven days. Friars enticed him away with fair

And for knowyng of comeres coped hym as a frere.   [600
Ac he hath leue to lepe out as oft as hym liketh,
And is welcome whan he wil and woneth wyth hem oft.
   Alle fledden for fere and flowen into hernes,
Saue Mede þe mayde, na mo durst abide.
Ac trewli to telle she trembled for drede,   [605
And ek wept and wronge whan she was attached.

words and, lest he should be recognised by chance-comers, dressed him up in a friar's habit. However, he has permission to go out whenever it pleases him, and is welcome when the fancy takes him and often stays with them.

They all ran away for fear and fled into hiding-places; not one of them dared to hold their ground except Lady Meed, and, indeed, she trembled with fright and wept and wrung her hands when she was arrested.

B

The kyng and his knightes to the kirke wente
To here matynes of þe day and þe masse after.
Þanne waked I of my wynkynge and wo was withalle
Þat I ne hadde sleped sadder and yseiȝen more.
Ac er I hadde faren a fourlonge feyntise me hente,   [5
That I ne myȝte ferther afoot for defaute of slepynge;
And sat softly adown and seide my bileue,
And so I babeled on my bedes, þei brouȝte me aslepe.
    And þanne saw I moche more þan I bifore tolde,
For I say þe felde ful of folke þat I bifore of seyde,   [10
And how Resoun gan arrayen hym alle þe reume to preche,
And with a crosse afor þe kynge comsed þus to techen.
    He preued þat þise pestilences were for pure synne,
And þe southwest wynde on Saterday at euene
Was pertliche for pure pryde and for no poynt elles.   [15
Piries and plomtrees were puffed to þe erthe,
In ensample, ȝe segges, ȝe shulden do þe bettere.
Beches and brode okes were blowen to þe grounde,
Torned vpward her tailles in tokenynge of drede
Þat dedly synne at domesday shal fordon hem alle.   [20
    Of þis matere I myȝte mamely ful longe,
Ac I shal seye as I saw, so me God helpe!
How pertly afor þe poeple Resoun gan to preche.
    He bad Wastoure go worche what he best couthe,
And wynnen his wastyng with somme manere crafte.   [25
And preyed Peronelle her purfyle to lete,
And kepe it in hir cofre for catel at hire nede.
Thomme Stowue he tauȝte to take two staues,
And fecche Felice home fro þe wyuen pyne.
    He warned Watt his wyf was to blame,   [30
Þat hire hed was worth halue a marke, his hode nouȝte worth
                                                        a grote.

And bad Bette kut a bow other tweyne,
And bete Betoun þerwith, but if she wolde worche.
And þanne he charged chapmen to chasten her childeren;
'Late no wynnynge hem forweny whil þei be ȝonge,   [35
Ne for no pouste of pestilence plese hem nouȝte out of resoun.
    My syre seyde so to me and so did my dame,
Þat þe leuere childe þe more lore bihoueth,

---

13 were: MS was   20 at: MS ar   29 Felice: MS filice

B: Sin and Repentance

The king and his knights went to church to hear Mattins of the day, followed by Mass. Then I awoke from my slumbers, grieving that I had not slept more soundly and seen more. However, before I had gone a few hundred yards I was overtaken by weakness, so that I could walk no further for lack of sleep. I sat down quietly and said the Creed and mumbled my prayers, which sent me to sleep.

Then I saw much more than I related before. I saw the meadow thronged with people, that I have already mentioned, and how Reason prepared to preach to all the people. Holding a cross, he began to teach in the king's presence in this fashion.

He showed that these outbreaks of plague were caused by sin alone, and that the south-westerly gale on Saturday evening clearly resulted simply and solely from pride. Pear-trees and plum-trees were dashed to the earth as an example to teach men to lead better lives. Beeches and broad oaks were blown to the ground and lay with their roots uppermost as a mark of fear that deadly sin shall bring them all to destruction on the Day of Judgment. I could make a long speech on this subject, but, with God's help, I will relate what I saw and how Reason preached plainly before the people.

He told spendthrifts to set to work at whatever job they understood best and to earn what they squandered by one trade or another. He requested vain Peronelle to discard her fine trimmings and put them away in her chest as a provision against time of need. He instructed Tom Stowe to take a couple of sticks and fetch Felicity home from the ducking-pond. He warned Walter that his wife should be blamed because her headdress was worth several shillings and his hood was worth less than a few coppers. He told Bartholomew to cut one or two branches and beat Betty with them if she refused to work. Then he cautioned tradesmen to discipline their children and not to spoil them when young by lavishing their gains upon them, nor indulge them immoderately because they lived under the menace of the plague, saying: 'My father told me, and my mother too, that the dearer the child, the more he needs training.' Solomon, who wrote the Book of Wisdom, said the same thing. The English version of the Latin text, for those who wish to know it, is: 'He who spares the rod hates his son.'

And Salamon seide þe same, þat Sapience made,
    Qui parcit virge, odit filium.
Þe Englich of þis Latyn is, whoso wil it knowe,   [40
Whoso spareth þe sprynge spilleth his children.'
   And sithen he preyed prelatz and prestes togideres,
'Þat 3e prechen to þe peple, preue it on 3owreseluen,
And doth it in dede, it shall drawe 3ow to good;
If 3e lyuen as 3e leren vs we shal leue 3ow þe bettere.'   [45
   And sithen he radde religioun here reule to holde—
'Leste þe kynge and his conseille 3owre comunes appayre,
And ben stuwardes of 3owre stedes til 3e be ruled bettre'.
   And sithen he conseilled þe kynge þe comune to louye:
'It is þi tresore, if tresoun ne were, and triacle at þi nede.'   [50
And sithen he prayed þe pope haue pite on holicherche,
And er he gyue any grace gouerne firste hymselue.
   'And 3e that han lawes to kepe, late treuthe be 3owre coueytise,
More þan golde or other gyftes, if 3e wil God plese;
For whoso contrarieth treuthe, he telleth in þe gospel,   [55
That God knoweth hym nou3te, ne no seynte of heuene,
    Amen dico vobis, nescio vos.
And 3e þat seke seynte Iames and seintes of Rome,
Seketh seynt Treuthe, for he may saue 3ow alle;
Qui cum patre et filio þat feire hem bifalle
Þat suweth my sermon'; and þus seyde Resoun.   [60
Thanne ran Repentance and reherced his teme,
And gert Wille to wepe water with his eyen. . . . .

Ira

Now awaketh Wratthe with two whyte eyen,
And nyuelynge with þe nose and his nekke hangynge.
   'I am Wrath', quod he, 'I was sum tyme a frere,   [65
And þe couentes gardyner for to graffe ympes;
On limitoures and listres lesynges I ymped,
Tyl þei bere leues of low speche lordes to plese,
And sithen þei blosmed obrode in boure to here shriftes.
And now is fallen þerof a frute þat folke han wel leuere   [70
Schewen her schriftes to hem þan shryue hem to her persones.
   And now persones han parceyued þat freres parte with hem,
Þise possessioneres preche and depraue freres,
And freres fyndeth hem in defaute, as folke bereth witnes,

⁷² han *supplied*

After that, he besought bishops and priests: 'Make manifest in yourselves what you preach to the people and carry it out in practice; it will be for your good. If you live in accordance with what you teach us, we shall the more readily believe you.'

Then he advised the religious orders to observe their Rule, 'lest the king and his council curtail your provisions and act as stewards in your houses until you are better governed'. After that, he counselled the king to cherish the common people: 'Failing treason, they are your treasure and a source of help for you in your time of need.' Next, he besought the Pope to have compassion on the church and first to govern himself before dispensing any grace. 'As for you whose task it is to uphold the law, if you wish to please God, let your desire be for truth rather than for gold or for other gifts, for He says in the Gospel that neither God nor any saint in heaven will acknowledge those who act against truth: "Truly, I say to you, I do not know you". And as for you who go to seek the shrines of St James and of saints of Rome, seek St Truth, for He can save you all, "who with the Father and the Son [liveth and reigneth, world without end, Amen]". May blessing be on those who follow my preaching!' So said Reason.

Repentance then came swiftly, repeating his theme, and caused the tears to flow from Will's eyes.

The confession of Anger

Now Anger bestirred himself, showing the whites of his eyes, with a snivelling nose and a hanging head.

'I am Anger', he said. 'Once upon a time, I was a friar. I was the gardener at the friary and my job was to graft shoots. I grafted lies onto the brothers who were licensed to beg round the district, and onto the preachers, until they bore leaves of obsequious speech to ingratiate themselves with men of rank, and subsequently spread their blossom widely in hearing confessions in ladies' apartments. Now the fruit of this has come, in that people would much rather make their confessions to them than to their parish priests. Since parish priests have realised that the friars are taking a share of their dues, the beneficed clergy revile the friars in their sermons, while the friars show *them* to be at fault, as anyone will testify. So, when they preach up and down the country, I, Anger, accompany them and prime them out of my books.

That whan þei preche þe poeple in many place aboute,   [75
I, Wrath, walke with hem and wisse hem of my bokes.
Þus þei speken of spiritualte þat eyther despiseth other,
Til þei be bothe beggers and by my spiritualte libben,
Or elles alle riche and riden aboute.
I, Wrath, rest neuere þat I ne moste folwe   [80
This wykked folke, for suche is my grace.
    I haue an aunte to nonne and an abbesse bothe,
Hir were leuere swowe or swelte þan soeffre any peyne.
I haue be cook in hir kichyne and þe couent serued
Many monthes with hem and with monkes bothe.   [85
I was þe priouresses potagere, and other poure ladyes,
And made hem ioutes of iangelynge, þat dame Iohanne was a
                                                              bastard,
And dame Clarice a kniȝtes douȝter, ac a kokewolde was hire syre,
And dame Peronelle a prestes file; priouresse worth she neuere,
For she had childe in chirityme, al owre chapitere it wiste.   [90
    Of wykked wordes I, Wrath, here wortes I made,
Til "þow lixte" and "þou lixte" lopen oute at ones,
And eyther hitte other vnder þe cheke;
Hadde þei had knyues, bi Cryst, her eyther had killed other.
    Seynt Gregorie was a gode pope and had a gode forwit,   [95
Þat no priouresse were prest for þat he ordeigned.
Þei had þanne ben *infamis* þe firste day, þei can so yuel hele conseille.
    Amonge monkes I miȝte be, ac many tyme I shonye;
For þere ben many felle frekis my feres to aspye,
Bothe prioure an supprioure and owre *pater abbas*;   [100
And if I telle any tales, þei taken hem togyderes,
And do me faste Frydayes to bred and to water,
And am chalanged in þe chapitelhous as I a childe were,
And baleised on þe bare ers, and no breche bitwene;
Forþi haue I no lykyng with þo leodes to wonye.   [105
I ete there vnthende fisshe and fieble ale drynke;
Ac other while, whan wyn cometh whan I drynke wyn at eue,
I haue a fluxe of a foule mouthe wel fyue dayes after.
Al þe wikkednesse þat I wote bi any of owre bretheren
I couth it in owre cloistre þat al owre couent wote it.'   [110
    'Now repent þe', quod Repentaunce, 'and reherce þow neure
Conseille þat þow cnowest bi contenaunce ne bi riȝte;
And drynke nouȝte ouer delicatly ne to depe noyther,
Þat þi wille bi cause þerof to wrath myȝte torne.
Esto sobrius', he seyde, and assoilled me after,   [115
And bad me wilne to wepe my wikkednesse to amende.

They talk about spiritual authority in such fashion that each pours scorn on the other, until both are brought to beggary and live according to *my* spiritual authority, or, alternatively, until they all grow rich and ride about on horseback. I, Anger, can never rest from following these wicked men, for that is the grace with which I am endowed.

'I have an aunt who is a nun and, what is more, an abbess. She would rather swoon or die than suffer any hardship. I have served many months as cook in the convent kitchen, among them, and among monks too. I was soup-maker to the prioress and to the other ladies vowed to poverty. I made their soups out of gossip that Sister Joan was a bastard and that Sister Clarice was the daughter of a knight, but her father was a cuckold, and that Sister Petronella was a priest's light-of-love. She could never be prioress, for, as all our chapter knew, she had a child in the cherry season. I, Anger, dressed their vegetables with evil words until "You're a liar!" and "*You're* a liar!" burst out simultaneously and each hit the other in the face. By heaven, if they had had knives, they would have killed each other. St Gregory was a good Pope and showed sound foresight in laying it down that no prioress might be made a priest. They are so bad at keeping confidences secret that they would have been guilty of infamous conduct from the very first.

'I could live among monks, but in general I avoid it, for there are many men of rigorous severity there—the prior and the sub-prior and our Father Abbot—to spy out my company. If I tell any tales, they take counsel together and make me fast on Fridays on bread and water. I am accused of my faults in the chapter house like a little boy and beaten on the bare buttocks with no breeches to cover me. So I do not enjoy living with those people. I get half-grown fish to eat there and thin ale to drink. However, at other times, when wine is served and I drink it in the evening, I spew up filth for a good five days afterwards. I publish in the cloister all the evil that I know concerning any of our brothers, so that the whole community comes to know it.'

'Now repent!' said Repentance. 'Never betray secrets, whether your knowledge of them comes by favour or as your right. Do not drink too luxuriously or too deeply, lest it should cause you to lust after anger. "Be sober!"' he said.

Then he gave me absolution and told me to desire to weep, to make amends for my sins.

Auaricia

And þanne cam Coueytise, can I hym nouȝte descryue
So hungriliche and holwe sire Heruy hym loked.
He was bitelbrowed and baberlipped also,
With two blered eyghen, as a blynde hagge;   [120
And as a letheren purs lolled his chekes,
Wel sydder þan his chyn þei chiueled for elde;
And as a bondman of his bacoun his berde was bidraueled.
With an hode on his hed, a lousi hatte aboue,
And in a tauny tabarde of twelue wynter age,   [125
Al totorne and baudy and ful of lys crepynge,
But if þat a lous couthe haue lopen þe bettre
She sholde nouȝte haue walked on þat welche, so was it thredebare.

'I haue ben coueytouse,' quod þis caityue, 'I biknowe it here;
For some tyme I serued Symme-atte-stile,   [130
And was his prentis ypliȝte, his profit to wayte.
First I lerned to lye a leef other tweyne,
Wikkedlich to weye was my furst lessoun.
To Wy and to Wynchestre I went to þe faire,
With many manere marchandise as my maistre me hiȝte;   [135
Ne had þe grace of gyle ygo amonge my ware,
It had be vnsolde þis seuene ȝere, so me God helpe!

Thanne drowe I me amonges draperes my donet to lerne,
To drawe þe lyser alonge, þe lenger it semed;
Amonge þe riche rayes I rendred a lessoun,   [140
To broche hem with a pak-nedle and plaited hem togyderes,
And put hem in a presse and pynned hem þerinne,
Tyl ten ȝerdes or twelue tolled out threttene.

My wyf was a webbe and wollen cloth made;
She spak to spynnesteres to spynnen it oute.   [145
Ac þe pounde þat she payed by poised a quarteroun more
Than myne owne auncere, whoso weyȝed treuthe.

I bouȝte hir barly-malte; she brewe it to selle,
Peny-ale and podyng-ale she poured togideres
For laboreres and for low folke; þat lay by hymselue.   [150
The best ale lay in my boure or in my bedchambre,
And whoso bummed þerof bouȝte it þerafter
A galoun for a grote, God wote, no lesse;
And ȝit it cam in cupmel; þis crafte my wyf vsed.

---

118 Heruy: MS Henri   141 pak-nedle: MS bat nedle   142 pynned: MS pyned
153 no: MS na

The confession of Avarice

Then Sir Harvey Covetousness came forward, looking so starved and gaunt that I cannot describe him. He had beetling brows and fleshy lips and eyes as bleary as a blind old woman's. His cheeks, trembling with age, hung right down below his chin, like a leather purse. His beard was all smeary with bacon grease, like a peasant's. He wore a hood on his head and a verminous hat on top of it, and a twelve-year-old tawny-coloured jacket, all tattered and dirty and full of creeping lice; though if any louse had been a better jumper, it would not have crawled on that stuff, it was so threadbare.

'I have been covetous', said this miserable wretch. 'I admit it here and now. At one time I worked for Simon-by-the-stile. I was his apprentice, bound by promise to keep an eye on his profits. First of all, I learned a page or two of lies, and my earliest lesson was in giving false weight. At my master's bidding, I went to the fairs at Weyhill and Winchester with a wide range of merchandise. If the grace of guile had not blessed my goods, God help me! they would have remained unsold these seven years!

'Then I took myself off to the drapers to learn my primer: how to tug at the selvage-edge to make it seem longer than it was. I put one lesson into practice among the costly striped fabrics, piercing them with a large needle and fastening them together, then putting them in a press and clamping them in it tightly until ten or twelve yards were stretched out to thirteen. My wife was a weaver who made woollen cloth. She hired spinners to spin it out. But the pound by which she paid them weighed a quarter more than my own scales, if true weight were given.

'I bought her barley-malt, which she brewed for sale. She mixed together thin ale and strong ale for labourers and the lower classes; that was kept on its own. The best ale was kept in my inner apartment or in my bedroom. Anyone who tasted it bought it afterwards at a groat a gallon, no less, God knows! But this was my wife's trick: even at that price, it was brought in a cupful at a time. She was known as Huckster Rose. All her life, she has been engaged in shady profit-making.

'But now, as I hope to prosper, I swear to forsake that sin and never to give false weight or sell my goods by crooked methods. I, and my wife too, will make a pilgrimage to

E

Rose þe regrater was hir riȝte name;   [155
She hath holden hokkerye al hire lyf-tyme.
  Ac I swere now, so the ik, þat synne wil I lete,
And neuere wikkedliche weye, ne wikke chaffare vse,
But wenden to Walsyngham, and my wyf als,
And bidde þe rode of Bromeholme brynge me oute of dette.'   [160
  'Repentedestow þe euere,' quod Repentance, 'ne restitucioun
                                       madest?'
  'Ʒus, ones I was herberwed', quod he, 'with an hep of chapmen,
I roos whan þei were arest and yrifled here males.'
  'That was no restitucioun,' quod Repentance, 'but a robberes
                                      thefte;
Þow haddest be better worthy be hanged þerfore   [165
Þan for al þat þat þow hast here shewed.'
  'I wende ryflynge were restitucioun,' quod he, 'for I lerned
                               neuere rede on boke,
And I can no Frenche, in feith, but of þe ferthest ende of Norfolke.'
  'Vsedestow euere vsurie', quod Repentaunce, 'in alle þi lyf-tyme?'
  'Nay, sothly,' he seyde, 'saue in my ȝouthe.   [170
I lerned amonge Lumbardes and Iewes a lessoun,
To wey pens with a peys and pare þe heuyest,
And lene it for loue of þe crosse, to legge a wedde and lese it;
Suche dedes I did wryte ȝif he his day breke,
I haue mo maneres þorw rerages þan þorw *miseretur et comodat*. [175
  I haue lent lordes and ladyes my chaffare,
And ben her brocour after and bouȝte it myself.
Eschaunges and cheuesances, with suche chaffare I dele,
And lene folke þat lese wol a lyppe at euery noble.
And with Lumbardes lettres I ladde golde to Rome,   [180
And toke it by taille here and tolde hem þere lasse.'
  'Lentestow euere lordes for loue of her mayntenaunce?'
  'Ʒe, I haue lent lordes loued me neuere after,
And haue ymade many a knyȝte bothe mercere and drapere,
Þat payed neuere for his prentishode nouȝte a peire gloues.' [185
  'Hastow pite on pore men þat mote nedes borwe?'
  'I haue as moche pite of pore men as pedlere hath of cattes,
Þat wolde kille hem, yf he cacche hem myȝte, for coueitise of here
                                    skynnes.'
  'Artow manlyche amonge þi neiȝbores of þi mete and drynke?'
  'I am holden', quod he, 'as hende as hounde is in kychyne,   [190

---

161 Repentedestow: MS Repentestow   165 be better: be *supplied*
182 Lentestow: MS Lenestow

Walsingham and pray that Bromholm Cross will bring me out of debt.'

'Did you ever repent, or make restitution?' Repentance asked.

'Yes', he said. 'There was one time when I shared a night's lodging with a lot of merchants. I got up while they were asleep and took the contents of their bags.'

'That was no restitution', said Repentance. 'It was theft and robbery. You deserve hanging for that, more than for all that you have just confessed.'

'I thought that robbery *was* restitution', he said. 'I am no scholar, and the only French I know is that spoken in the outlying parts of Norfolk.'

'Did you ever at any time resort to usury?' Repentance asked.

'No, truly,' he said, 'except in my young days. I learned from Lombards and Jews the trick of balancing coins against a weight in the scale-pan, and clipping the heaviest. I would lend these for love of the cross they bore, in exchange for a pledge which the borrower stood to lose; I drew up such tight contracts to cover failure to repay by the proper date. I have acquired more manors as a result of people falling into arrears than I ever have by behaving as one who "deals generously and lends". I have lent my wares to lords and ladies and afterwards acted as their broker and bought the goods myself. I deal in exchanges and loan-agreements and similar commodities; those to whom I lend can be sure of a part-loss on every gold coin. I got money to Rome by means of letters of credit from the Lombards. The amount that I took was recorded by a tally here, but I paid less there than the amount due.'

'Did you ever lend money to lords to win their backing for your misdeeds?'

'Oh yes, I have lent money to lords; they never loved me for it afterwards. I have made mercers and drapers out of many knights who never paid so much as a pair of gloves for their apprenticeship.'

'Do you show any pity to the poor who have to borrow through necessity?'

'I have as much pity for the poor as a pedlar has for cats; if he managed to catch them, he would kill them to get their pelts.'

'Are you generous to your neighbours with your food and drink?'

Amonges my neighbores, namelich, such a name ich haue.'
    'Now God leue neure,' quod Repentance, 'but þow repent þe
                                                        rather,
Þe grace on þis grounde þi good wel to bisette,
Ne þine ysue after þe haue ioye of þat þow wynnest,
Ne þi ex-cecutours wel bisett þe siluer þat þow hem leuest;   [195
And þat was wonne with wronge, with wikked men be despended.
For were I frere of þat hous þere gode faith and charite is,
I nolde cope vs with þi catel, ne owre kyrke amende,
Ne haue a peny to my pitaunce of þyne, bi my soule hele,
For þe best boke in owre house, þeiȝe brent golde were þe leues,
                                                        [200

And I wyst wytterly þow were suche as þow tellest.
    Seruus es alterius cum fercula pinguia queris,
    Pane tuo pocius vescere, liber eris.
    Thow art an vnkynde creature, I can þe nouȝte assoille
Til þow make restitucioun and rekne with hem alle,   [205
And sithen þat resoun rolle it in þe regystre of heuene
That þow hast made vche man good, I may þe nouȝte assoille;
    Non dimittitur peccatum donec restituatur ablatum, etc.
For alle þat haue of þi good, haue God my trouthe!
Ben holden at þe heighe dome to helpe þe to restitue.
And whoso leueth nouȝte þis be soth, loke in þe sauter glose, [210
In *miserere mei deus* where I mene treuthe,
    Ecce enim veritatem dilexisti, etc.
Shal neuere werkman in þis worlde þryue wyth þat þow wynnest;
Cum sancto sanctus eris; construe me þat on Englische.'
    Thanne wex þat shrewe in wanhope and walde haue hanged
                                                        himself,
Ne hadde Repentaunce þe rather reconforted hym in þis manere:
                                                        [215

'Haue mercye in þi mynde and with þi mouth biseche it,
For Goddes mercye is more þan alle hise other werkes;
    Misericordia eius super omnia opera eius, etc.
    And al þe wikkednesse in þis worlde þat man myȝte worche
                                                        or thynke,
Ne is no more to þe mercye of God þan in þe see a glede;
    *Omnis iniquitas quantum ad misericordiam dei, est quasi sintilla in
                                                medio maris.*
    Forþi haue mercy in þi mynde, and marchandise, leue it,   [220

---

²⁰¹ tellest: MS telleth   ²⁰⁸ þat haue: MS þat hath   ²⁰⁹ Ben: MS Is
²¹⁹ *quasi supplied*

'I am thought to show as much courtesy as a dog in a kitchen', he said. 'Among my neighbours, in particular, that is my reputation.'

Repentance said: 'Unless you repent quickly, God grant that you may never have grace to employ your wealth to good purpose in this world, nor your children after you enjoy what you have accumulated, nor your executors make good use of the money you leave them; and may wicked men have the spending of that which was acquired by wrong-doing! For if I were a friar in a house where good faith and love prevailed, I would not provide copes for us with any money of yours, nor repair our church, nor take a penny for my own share, I swear, not for the finest book in our house, not even if its leaves were of burnished gold, if I knew for certain that you were such a man as you make yourself out to be, for: "Thou art the slave of another, when thou seekest after dainty dishes; feed rather upon bread of thine own, and thou wilt be a free man." You are devoid of natural feeling; I am powerless to absolve you. Until you make restitution and satisfy them all; and until Reason has entered in the records of heaven that you have made good what is owing to all men, I cannot give you absolution. "Sin is not remitted until restitution is made." And, as God is my witness, all those who have received a share of your wealth are required to help you make restitution at the great Judgment.

'If anyone doubts the truth of what I say, let him consult the commentary on the verse: "Behold, thou desirest truth in the inward being" in the Psalm "Have mercy on me, O God". No man living will ever thrive on what is gained by you. Ponder the meaning of the words: "With the pure thou dost show thyself pure [and with the crooked thou dost show thyself perverse]".'

At that, the miserable wretch lapsed into despair and would have hanged himself if Repentance had not made haste to comfort him, saying: 'Fix your thoughts on mercy, and implore it with your tongue, for God's mercy surpasses all His other acts: "His compassion is over all that he has made." And, as has also been said, "All the evil [that may be done or thought on earth] is no greater, in comparison with the mercy of God, than a spark in the sea." So keep mercy in mind, and as for your buying and selling, give it up! You have no good source from which to get yourself so much as a

For þow hast no good grounde to gete þe with a wastel,
But if it were with thi tonge or ellis with þi two hondes.
For þe good þat þow hast geten bigan al with falsehede,
And as longe as þow lyuest þerwith þow ȝeldest nouȝte, but
                                         borwest.
And if þow wite neuere to whiche ne whom to restitue,   *[225*
Bere it to þe bisschop and bidde hym, of his grace,
Bisette it hymselue as best is for þi soule.
For he shal answere for þe at þe heygh dome,
For þe and for many mo þat man shal ȝif a rekenynge.
What he lerned ȝow in lente, leue þow none other,   *[230*
And what he lent ȝow of owre Lordes good to lette ȝow fro
                               synne.' . . . .

And þanne had Repentaunce reuthe and redde hem alle to knele,
'For I shal biseche for al synful owre saueoure of grace
To amende vs of owre mysdedes and do mercy to vs alle.
Now God,' quod he, 'þat of þi goodnesse gonne þe worlde make,
                                    [235
And of nauȝte madest auȝte and man moste liche to þiselue,
And sithen suffredest for to synne, a sikenesse to vs alle,
And al for þe best, as I bileue, what euere þe boke telleth,
     O felix culpa! o necessarium peccatum Ade! &c.
For þourgh þat synne þi sone sent was to þis erthe,
And bicam man of a mayde, mankynde to saue,   *[240*
And madest þiself with þi sone and vs synful yliche,
     Faciamus hominem ad ymaginem et similitudinem nostram;
     Et alibi: qui manet in caritate, in deo manet, et deus in eo;
And sith with þiself sone in owre sute deydest
On Gode Fryday for mannes sake at ful tyme of þe daye,
Þere þiself ne þi sone no sorwe in deth feledest;
But in owre secte was þe sorwe and þi sone it ladde,   *[245*
     Captiuam duxit captiuitatem.
Þe sonne for sorwe þerof les syȝte for a tyme
Aboute myddday, whan most liȝte is and mele tyme of seintes;
Feddest with þi fresche blode owre forfadres in derknesse,
     Populus qui ambulabat in tenebris, vidit lucem magnam;
And thorw þe liȝte þat lepe oute of þe Lucifer was blent,
And blewe alle þi blissed into þe blisse of paradise.   *[250*
Þe thrydde daye after þow ȝedest in owre sute,
A synful Marie þe seighe ar seynte Marie þi dame,
And al to solace synful þow suffredest it so were;
     Non veni vocare iustos, set peccatores ad penitenciam.

loaf of bread, except your tongue and your two hands. The wealth you have amassed came from falsehood in the first place, and as long as you live on it, you are not paying, but borrowing. If you do not know to which one or to whom restitution should be made, take the money to the bishop, and ask him as a favour to use it as he thinks fit, for the greatest good of your soul. For rest assured that he will have to answer for you, and for many others besides you, on the Day of Judgment, and give account of what he taught you during Lent, and what he gave you from among the riches of our Lord to keep you from sin.'

Then Repentance took pity on them and told them all to kneel down, saying: 'I will pray to our Saviour on behalf of all sinners to give us grace to mend our sinful ways and to show mercy on us all.'

'O God,' he said, 'who, in Your goodness, made the world, creating all things out of nothing and man nearest in likeness to Yourself, and afterwards allowed him to fall into sin, which infects us all (and yet, I believe, all was for the best, whatever the book may say: "O joyful fault! O necessary sin of Adam!" For on account of that sin Your Son was sent to this earth and was made man, born of a virgin, to save mankind.) And through Your Son You brought Yourself and us sinful men into one likeness, as the Bible records: "Let us make man in our image, after our likeness" and, in another place: "He who abides in love abides in God, and God abides in him." Afterwards, in the person of Your Son Himself, clad in the garment of our flesh, You died for man's sake on Good Friday at high noon. Neither You nor Your Son then experienced the sorrow of death; it was in our flesh that the sorrow was felt, and Your Son conquered it; He "led captivity captive".

'For grief at this the sun lost its sight for a while at midday— the time when light is greatest and the holy receive refreshment. At that hour You fed our forefathers in the darkness of hell with Your fresh blood, and "the people who walked in darkness have seen a great light". Lucifer was blinded by the light that sprang out of You, and like a wind You swept Your blessed ones into the joy of Paradise. The third day afterwards You went about in our flesh. A sinful Mary saw You before St Mary Your mother; You allowed this to be so to hearten sinners, for, as You said: "I came not to call the righteous, but sinners [to repentance]." All Your most valiant deeds, re-

And al þat Marke hath ymade, Mathew, Iohan, and Lucas,
Of þyne douȝtiest dedes were don in owre armes;   [255
    Verbum caro factum est, et habitauit in nobis.
And bi so moche, me semeth, þe sikerere we mowe
Bydde and biseche, if it be þi wille,
Þat art owre fader and owre brother, be merciable to vs,
And haue reuthe on þise ribaudes þat repente hem here sore,
Þat euere þei wratthed þe in þis worlde in worde, þouȝte,
                              or dedes.'   [260

Þanne hent Hope an horne of *deus, tu conuersus viuificabis,*
And blew it with *beati quorum remisse sunt iniquitates,*
Þat alle seyntes in heuene songen at ones,
    Homines et iumenta saluabis, quemadmodum multiplicasti miseri-
                                cordiam tuam, deus, etc.

    A thousand of men þo thrungen togyderes;
Criede vpward to Cryst and to his clene moder   [265
To haue grace to go with hem Treuthe to seke.
    Ac þere was wyȝte non so wys þe wey þider couthe,
But blustreden forth as bestes ouer bankes and hilles,
Til late was and longe þat þei a lede mette,
Apparailled as a paynym in pylgrymes wyse.   ·   [270
He bare a burdoun ybounde with a brode liste,
In a withewyndes wise ywounden aboute.
A bolle and a bagge he bare by his syde;
An hundreth of ampulles on his hatt seten,
Signes of Synay and shelles of Galice;   [275
And many a cruche on his cloke, and keyes of Rome,
And þe vernicle bifore, for men shulde knowe,
And se bi his signes whom he souȝte hadde.
    Þis folke frayned hym firste fro whennes he come.
'Fram Synay,' he seyde 'and fram owre Lordes sepulcre;   [280
In Bethleem and in Babiloyne I haue ben in bothe,
In Ermonye, in Alisaundre, in many other places.
Ȝe may se bi my signes þat sitten on myn hatte,
Þat I haue walked ful wyde in wete and in drye,
And souȝte gode seyntes for my soules helth.'   [285
    'Knowestow ouȝte a corseint þat men calle Treuthe?
Coudestow auȝte wissen vs þe weye where þat wy dwelleth?'
    'Nay, so me God helpe!' seide þe gome þanne,
'I seygh neuere palmere with pike ne with scrippe
Axen after hym er til now in þis place.'   [290
    'Peter!' quod a plowman, and put forth his hed,
'I knowe hym as kyndely as clerke doþ his bokes;

corded by Mark and Matthew, John and Luke, were done in the armour of our flesh: "The Word became flesh, and dwelt among us." Therefore, it seems to me, we may the more confidently pray and implore You, who are our Father and our Brother, to be merciful to us, if it be Your will, and to have pity on these sinners who now bitterly repent that they ever in their lives angered You by word or thought or deeds.'

Then Hope seized a horn made of "O God, thou wilt revive [me] again", and blew on it the notes of "Blessed is he whose transgression is forgiven", so that all the saints in heaven began to sing: "Man and beast thou savest, O Lord. How precious is thy steadfast love, O God! [The children of men take refuge in the shadow of thy wings]."

Then a thousand people crowded together, sending their prayer up to Christ and His pure mother that grace might accompany them in their search for Truth.

However, there was no one knowledgeable enough to know the way, so they went blundering about like cattle over banks and hills until, at long last, they met a man dressed, pilgrim-fashion, like a Saracen. He carried a staff bound with a strip of broad cloth selvage, wound round it like bindweed. He carried a begging-bowl and a bag at his side. Many phials of holy water, and pilgrim's badges from Sinai, and scallop shells from Galicia, were fixed to his hat. He also had emblems of the Cross from the Holy Land sewn to his cloak, and the cross-keys of Rome, and a handkerchief of St Veronica in front, so that, by sight of his badges, it might be known which shrines he had visited.

First, the people asked him whence he came.

'From Sinai,' he said, 'and from our Lord's sepulchre. I have been in Bethlehem and Babylon and Armenia and Alexandria and many other places. You can see from the tokens on my hat that I have trudged a long way, in rain and shine, seeking the shrines of holy saints for the good of my soul.'

'Do you know anything about a saint called Truth? Could you by any means set us on the way to his dwelling?'

'God help me, no!' the man replied. 'Until here and now, I have never known any palmer, with his staff and his scrip, enquire about him.'

'By St Peter!' said a ploughman, shouldering his way forward, 'I know him as intimately as a scholar knows his books. Conscience and Natural Intelligence taught me the

Conscience and Kynde Witte kenned me to his place,
And deden me suren hym sikerly to serue hym for euere,
Bothe to sowe and to sette þe while I swynke myghte.   *[295*
I haue ben his folwar al þis fourty wyntre;
Bothe ysowen his sede and sued his bestes,
Withinne and withouten wayted his profyt.
I dyke and I delue, I do þat Treuthe hoteth;
Some tyme I sowe and some tyme I thresche,   *[300*
In tailoures crafte and tynkares crafte what Treuthe can deuyse,
I weue an I wynde and do what Treuthe hoteth.
For, þouȝe I seye it myself, I serue hym to paye.
Ich haue myn huire of hym wel and otherwhiles more;
He is þe prestest payer þat pore men knoweth;   *[305*
He ne with-halt non hewe his hyre þat he ne hath it at euen.
He is as low as a lombe and loueliche of speche,
And ȝif ȝe wilneth to wite where þat he dwelleth,
I shal wisse ȝow witterly þe weye to his place.'
   'Ȝe, leue Pieres', quod þis pilgrymes, and profered hym huire *[310*
For to wende with hem to Treuthes dwellyng-place.
'Nay, bi my soules helth,' quod Pieres, and gan forto swere,
'I nolde fange a ferthynge for seynt Thomas shryne!
Treuthe wolde loue me þe lasse a longe tyme þereafter!
   Ac if ȝe wilneth to wende wel, þis is þe weye thider: *[315*
Ȝe mote go þourgh Mekenesse, bothe men and wyues,
Tyl ȝe come into Conscience, þat Cryst wite þe sothe,
Þat ȝe louen owre Lorde God leuest of alle þinges,
And þanne ȝowre neighbores nexte in non wise apeyre
Otherwyse þan þow woldest he wrouȝte to þiselue.   *[320*
   And so boweth forth bi a broke, Beth-buxum-of-speche,
Tyl ȝe fynden a forth, Ȝowre-fadres-honoureth,
      Honora patrem et matrem, &c.
Wadeþ in þat water and wascheth ȝow wel þere,
And ȝe shul lepe þe liȝtloker al ȝowre lyf-tyme.
And so shaltow se Swere-nouȝte-but-if-it-be-for-nede-   *[325*
And-namelich-an-ydel-þe-name-of-God-almyȝti.
   Þanne shaltow come by a crofte, but come þow nouȝte þereinne;
That crofte hat Coueyte-nouȝte-mennes-catel-ne-her-wyues-
Ne-none-of-her-seruauntes-þat-noyen-hem-myȝte;
Loke ȝe breke no bowes þere, but if it be ȝowre owne.   *[330*
   Two stokkes þere stondeth, ac stynte ȝe nouȝte þere,
They hatte Stele-nouȝte, ne-slee-nouȝte; stryke forth by bothe;

---

³⁰⁴ of hym *supplied*   ³³² hatte: MS hat

way to his dwelling-place and made me solemnly swear to
serve him for ever, sowing and planting for him as long as I
am able to work. I have followed him for forty years, sowing
his seed and keeping his cattle, watching over his profits
indoors and out of doors. I ditch and delve and obey Truth's
orders. Sometimes I sow, sometimes I thresh; I work as a
tailor or a tinker, carrying out Truth's plans. I weave and spin
and do whatever he bids me. Although I say it myself, I
serve him to his satisfaction. He gives me good wages, and
something over at times; he is the promptest payer that the
poor can have and never holds back a servant's earnings
overnight. He is as unassuming as a lamb, and his words are
full of kindness. If you want to know where he lives, I can
tell you exactly how to get there.'

'Yes, please, good Piers', said these pilgrims, and offered
him money to go with them to Truth's dwelling-place.

'Not as I value my soul!' said Piers, and swore: 'I would
not take a farthing, not for all the treasure in St Thomas's
shrine! Truth would love me the less for a long time after-
wards! But if you want your journey to be successful, this is
the way to get there.

'Men and women alike, you must make your way through
Meekness until you come to Conscience, so that Christ may
know that you truly love the Lord our God more dearly than
anything, and then, next to Him, your neighbours, not
injuring them in any way or acting towards them otherwise
than you would wish them to act towards you. Then turn
along by a brook called Be-mild-of-speech, until you come to
a ford, Honour-your-fathers: "Honour thy father and thy
mother, etc." Wade into that water, and wash yourselves well
in it, and you will be the more light of foot for the rest of
your lives. Then you will see Do-not-swear-except-in-
necessity-and-especially-do-not-take-the-name-of-Almighty-
God-in-vain. Next, you will come to a field, but do not go
into it. The field is called Thou-shalt-not-covet-thy-neigh-
bours'-cattle-nor-their-wives-nor-any-of-their-servants-to-
cause-them-injury. Mind that you break no branches there,
unless they belong to you. A pair of stocks stand there, but do
not linger by them. They are called Thou-shalt-not-steal and
Thou-shalt-do-no-murder. Pass along by both of them,

And leue hem on þi left halfe and loke nouȝte þereafter;
And holde wel þyne haliday heighe til euen.

 Thanne shaltow blenche at a berghe Bere-no-false-witnesse, *[335*
He is frithed in with floreines and other fees many;
Loke þow plukke no plante þere, for peril of þi soule.

 Þanne shal ȝe se Sey-soth-so-it-be-to-done-
In-no-manere-ellis-nauȝte-for-no-mannes-biddynge.

 Þanne shaltow come to a courte as clere as þe sonne, *[340*
Þe mote is of Mercy, þe manere aboute,
And alle þe wallis ben of Witte, to holden Wille oute;
And kerneled with Crystendome, mankynde to saue,
Boterased with Bileue-so-or-þow-beest-nouȝte-ysaued.

 And alle þe houses ben hiled, halles and chambres, *[345*
With no lede, but with Loue and Lowe-speche-as-bretheren.
Þe brugge is of Bidde-wel-þe-bette-may-þow-spede;
Eche piler is of Penaunce, of preyeres to seyntes,
Of Almes-dedes ar þe hokes þat þe gates hangen on.

 Grace hatte þe gateward, a gode man forsothe, *[350*
Hys man hatte Amende-ȝow, for many man him knoweth;
Telleth hym þis tokene, þat Treuthe wite þe sothe;
"I parfourned þe penaunce þe preest me enioyned,
And am ful sori for my synnes, and so I shal euere,
Whan I þinke þere-on, þeighe I were a pope." *[355*

 Biddeth Amende-ȝow meke him til his maistre ones,
To wayue vp þe wiket þat þe womman shette,
Tho Adam and Eue eten apples vnrosted;
  Per Euam cunctis clausa est, et par Mariam virginem iterum
              patefacta est;
For he hath þe keye and þe clikat, þouȝ þe kynge slepe.

 And if Grace graunte þe to go in in þis wise, *[360*
Þow shalt see in þiselue Treuthe sitte in þine herte,
In a cheyne of charyte, as þow a childe were,
To suffre hym and segge nouȝte aȝein þi sires wille.

 Ac bewar þanne of Wrath-þe, þat is a wikked shrewe,
He hath enuye to hym þat in þine herte sitteth; *[365*
And pukketh forþ pruyde to prayse þiseluen.
Þe boldnesse of þi bienfetes maketh þe blynde þanne,
And þanne worstow dryuen oute as dew, and þe dore closed,
Kayed and clikated, to kepe þe withouten;
Happily an hundreth wyntre ar þow eft entre. *[370*
Þus myght þow lesen his loue to late wel by þiselue,

---

336 fees: MS foes **346** With: MS Wit **358** *cunctis:* MS *cuntis; iterum supplied*

leaving them on your left, and do not look back at them; and
keep the Sabbath in full holiness until the close of day.

'You must turn aside when you come to a hill called Thou-
shalt-not-bear-false-witness, which is hedged round with
florins and many other kinds of bribe. Take care not to
gather any plants there, lest you imperil your soul. Then you
will see Speak-the-truth-as-is-your-duty-and-nothing-else-
but-truth-at-any-man's-request.

'Then you will come to a mansion as bright as the sun. The
moat round the estate is made of Mercy, and all the walls are
built of Reason, to keep out Self-Will, with battlements of
Christendom, to save mankind, buttressed with Believe-thus-
or-you-will-not-be-saved. All the buildings, both halls and
chambers, are roofed, not with lead, but with Love and
Meek-brotherly-speech. The drawbridge is made of Pray-well-
that-you-may-fare-the-better, and all the pillars of penance
and prayers to the saints; the hinges on which the gates are
hung are made of almsgiving. The gatekeeper, a good man,
is called Grace and his servant, who is widely known, is called
Amendment. Tell him this password, so that Truth may
know the true facts:

' "I have done the penance that the priest gave me, and I
am deeply sorry for my sins and always shall be when I
think of them, even if I became Pope."

'Ask Amendment to make a humble plea to his master to
open the wicket-gate which the woman shut when Adam
and Eve ate unroasted apples: "Through Eve it was closed
to all, and through the Virgin Mary it was opened again."
For he has the key of the latch, even when the king is sleeping.
And if Grace permits you to enter thus, you will find Truth
dwelling within your own heart, bound fast in charity, as if
you were a child, submissive to him and never gainsaying
your father's will.

'But beware then of Wrath, who is evil and wicked. He is
jealous of him that dwells in your heart, and thrusts pride
forward, to fill you with self-praise. Confidence in your good
deeds will blind you, and then you will be driven out like dew
and the door will be closed, locked and latched to keep you
outside; a hundred years might pass before you could come in
again. So you could lose his love through thinking much of
yourself and perhaps never enter again, unless you are given
grace.

And neuere happiliche efte entre, but grace þow haue.

Ac þere aren seuene sustren þat seruen Treuthe euere,
And aren porteres of þe posternes that to þe place longeth.
Þat one hat Abstenence, and Humilite an other,   [375
Charite and Chastite ben his chief maydenes,
Pacience and Pees, moche poeple þei helpeth,
Largenesse þe lady heo let in ful manye;
Heo hath hulpe a þousande oute of þe deueles ponfolde.
And who is sibbe to þis seuene, so me God helpe!   [380
He is wonderliche welcome and faire vnderfongen.
And but-if ȝe be syb to summe of þise seuene,
It is ful harde, bi myne heued', quod Peres, 'for any of ȝow alle
To geten ingonge at any gate þere, but grace be þe more.'

    'Now, bi Cryst', quod a cutpurs, 'I haue no kynne þere!'   [385
'Ne I,' quod an apewarde, 'bi auȝte þat I knowe!'
'Wite God,' quod a wafrestre, 'wist I þis for sothe,
Shulde I neuere ferthere a fote for no freres prechynge.'

    'Ȝus,' quod Pieres þe plowman, and pukked hem alle to gode,
'Mercy is a maydene þere hath myȝte ouer hem alle;   [390
And she is syb to alle synful and her sone also;
And þoruȝe þe helpe of hem two (hope þow none other),
Þow myȝte gete grace þere, bi so þow go bityme.'

    'By seynt Poule,' quod a pardonere, 'perauenture I be nouȝte
                                              knowe þere,
I wil go fecche my box with my breuettes and a bulle with
                                        bisshopes lettres!'   [395
'By Cryst,' quod a comune womman, 'þi companye wil I folwe,
Þow shalt sey I am þi sustre.' I ne wot where þei bicome.

---

³⁷³ aren: MS ar

'However, there are seven sisters who serve Truth perpetually; they are doorkeepers of that mansion. One is called Abstinence, another is called Humility; his principal maid servants are Charity and Chastity. Patience and Peace give help to a multitude of people, and the lady Generosity, who has assisted thousands out of the devil's pound, lets many in. As God is my helper, anyone who is related to these seven is given a great welcome and a courteous reception, but if you are not related to some of the seven', Piers said, 'I promise you it will be very difficult for any of you to gain entrance at any of the gates, unless additional grace and favour is shown to you.'

'By Christ! I have no relations there,' said a cutpurse.

'Nor I,' said an entertainer leading an ape, 'so far as I know.'

'If I were sure this was true, God knows I would not go a foot further, no matter what any friar said in his sermon,' said a baker's wife.

'Yes, you have!' said Piers the Ploughman, urging them all on to goodness. 'There is a maiden there called Mercy, who has power over them all, and she, and her Son also, are related to all sinners. You can be sure that, by the help of those two, you can receive grace there, if you go quickly.'

'By St Paul!' said a Pardoner, 'it may be that I am not known there. I will go and get my box of indulgences, and my papal Bull, and my bishop's letters.'

'By Christ!' said a woman of the streets, 'I will go along in your company. You can say that I am your sister.'

What happened to them, I do not know.

C

I lay down longe in þis þouȝte and atte laste I slepte,
And, as Cryste wolde, þere come Conscience to conforte me
þat tyme,
And bad me come to his courte, with Clergye sholde I dyne.
And for Conscience of Clergye spake I come wel þe rather,
And þere I say a maistre, what man he was I neste,   [5
Þat lowe louted and loueliche to Scripture.
Conscience knewe hym wel and welcomed hym faire;
Þei wesshen and wypeden and wenten to þe dyner.
Ac Pacience in þe paleis stode in pilgrymes clothes,
And preyde mete for charite for a pore heremyte.   [10
Conscience called hym in and curteisliche seide:
'Welcome, wye, go and wasshe; þow shalt sitte sone.'
    Þis maister was made sitte as for þe moste worthy,
And þanne Clergye and Conscience and Pacience cam after.
Pacience and I were put to be macches,   [15
And seten by owre selue at a syde borde.
Conscience called after mete, and þanne cam Scripture,
And serued hem þus sone of sondry metes manye
Of Austyn, of Ambrose, of alle þe foure euangelistes;
    Edentes & bibentes que apud eos sunt.
Ac þis maister ne his man no manere flesshe eten,   [20
Ac þei ete mete of more coste, mortrewes and potages;
Of þat men mys-wonne þei made hem wel at ese.
Ac her sauce was ouer-soure and vnsauourely grounde
In a morter, *post-mortem*, of many bitter peyne,
But if þei synge for þo soules and wepe salt teres: [25
    Vos qui peccata hominum comeditis, nisi pro eis lacrimas et orationes
    effunderitis, ea que in delicijs comeditis, in tormetntis euometis.
Conscience ful curteisly þo comaunded Scripture
Bifor Pacience bred to brynge, and me þat was his macche.
He sette a soure lof to-for vs and seyde: '*agite penitenciam*',
And sith he drough vs drynke *diu-perseuerans*.
'As longe', quod I, 'as I lyue and lycame may dure!'   [30
'Here is propre seruice,' quod Pacience, 'þer fareth no prynce
bettere';
And þanne he brouȝt vs forth a mees of other mete, of *Miserere-*
mei-deus;
And he brouȝte vs of *Beati-quorum*, of *Beatus-virres* makynge,

---

¹² wye: MS wyel ȝe   ²⁹ *diu:* MS dia

C: Through Patience to Love

I lay for a long time turning over these thoughts, and finally I fell asleep. Then, as Christ would have it, Conscience came to hearten me and invited me to his palace to dine with Learning. Since Conscience mentioned Learning, I went much more readily, and there I saw a Master of Divinity—I did not know who he was—who bowed to Scripture with befitting reverence. Conscience knew him well and gave him a warm welcome. They washed and dried themselves and went in to dinner. However, Patience, dressed as a pilgrim, stood in the palace entrance-hall desiring food, of their charity, for a poor hermit. Conscience bade him come in and said courteously: 'Welcome, my friend. Go and wash, and then you shall sit down at once.' The Master of Divinity was settled down in the seat of honour, and then Learning, Conscience and Patience followed. Patience and I were placed as partners, sitting on our own at a side table.

Conscience called for food, and then Scripture came and promptly served them with a wide variety of dishes made from the writings of St Augustine and St Ambrose and the four Evangelists; in St Luke's words, 'eating and drinking what they provide'. The Master of Divinity and his servant, however, ate no meat of any kind, but the food that they did eat was more costly: pâtés and thick soups. They made themselves very comfortable on things that people had not come by honestly. Yet the sauce to their food was over-sour and unappetising, being ground in the mortar of bitter torments to come after death, if they fail to sing the Offices for the souls of those people and to shed tears for them: 'O you who devour the sins of men, unless you pour forth tears and prayers for them, that which you eat in pleasure, you shall vomit up in torment.'

Then, with much courtesy, Conscience instructed Scripture to bring bread for Patience and for me, his table companion. He set a sour loaf in front of us, saying 'Repent!' then drew us a draught of Long-continued-enduring. 'For as long as I live and my body may last', I said. 'This is fine service', said Patience. 'There is not a prince who fares better.'

Then he produced another dish for us. This was the food of the Psalms: 'Have mercy on me, O God' and 'Blessed is he [whose transgression is forgiven]', made by 'Blessed is the man [to whom the Lord imputes no iniquity], and whose sin

Et-quorum-tecta-sunt-peccata in a disshe
Of derne shrifte, *Dixi* and *confitebor tibi*!
'Brynge Pacience some pitaunce', pryueliche quod Conscience;   [35
And þanne had Pacience a pitaunce, *pro-hac-orabit-ad-te-omnis-*
                                       sanctus-in-tempore-oportuno;
And Conscience conforted vs and carped vs mery tales,
    Cor contritum et humiliatum, deus, non despicies.
    Pacience was proude of þat propre seruice,
And made hym muirth with his mete, ac I morned euere,   [40
For þis doctoure on þe heigh dese dranke wyn so faste;
    Ve vobis qui potentes estis ad bibendum vinum!
He eet many sondry metes, mortrewes and puddynges,
Wombe-cloutes and wylde braune & egges yfryed with grece.
Þanne seide I to myself, so Pacience it herde,
'It is nouȝt foure dayes þat þis freke, bifor þe den of Poules,   [45
Preched of penaunces þat Poule þe apostle suffred,
In fame & frigore and flappes of scourges;
    Ter cesus sum, et a iudeis quinquies quadragenas, &c.
    Ac o worde þei ouerhuppen at ech a tyme þat þei preche,
Þat Poule in his pistel to al þe peple tolde;
    Periculum est in falsis fratribus.
Holywrit bit men be war; I wil nouȝt write it here   [50
On Englisch, an auenture it sholde be reherced to ofte,
And greue þerewith þat good men ben, ac gramarienes shul rede;
    Vnusquisque a fratre se custodiat, quia, vt dicitur, periculum est in
                                              falsis fratribus.
    Ac I wist neuere freke þat as a frere ȝede bifor men on Englisshe
Taken it for her teme and telle it withouten glosynge.
Þei prechen þat penaunce is profitable to þe soule,   [55
And what myschief and malese Cryst for man tholed;
Ac þis Goddes gloton', quod I, 'with his gret chekes,
Hath no pyte on vs pore; he performeth yuel;
Þat he precheth, he preueth nouȝt', to Pacience I tolde,
And wisshed witterly with wille ful egre   [60
Þat disshes and dobleres bifor þis ilke doctour
Were molten led in his maw, and Mahoun amyddes!
'I shal iangle to þis Iurdan, with his iust wombe,
To telle me what penaunce is, of which he preched rather.'—
Pacience perceyued what I thouȝt and wynked on me to be stille,
                                                            [65

---

⁶⁰ ful: MS for *corrected in margin to* ful   ⁶¹ and: MS a
⁶² molten: MS moltoun

is covered', on a plate of privy confession, 'I said [I will confess my transgressions to the Lord], and 'I acknowledged my sin to thee'. Conscience said, in an aside: 'Bring Patience a share!' and then Patience was given a helping of 'Therefore let every one who is godly offer prayer to thee at a time of distress'. Conscience encouraged us, telling us the joyful tale: 'A broken and contrite heart, O God, thou wilt not despise'.

Patience was very gratified by the good service and enjoyed his food, but all the time I was lamenting because this doctor up on the high dais drank his wine so fast: 'Woe to those who are heroes at drinking wine!' He ate many different dishes: pâtés, puddings, tripe, brawn made from the flesh of wild boars, and eggs fried in fat. Then I said to myself, letting Patience hear me: 'It is less than four days since this man preached before the Dean of St Paul's about the penances undergone by the Apostle Paul "in hunger and in cold" and lashed by scourges. "Three times I have been beaten with rods", he says; and "five times I have received at the hands of the Jews the forty lashes [less one]". But every time they preach they skip one detail which Paul made known in his epistle to all his readers, namely, "danger from false brethren". Holy Scripture gives the warning: "Let each man be on his guard against his brother, since, as it is said, there is danger in false brethren". (I am reluctant to translate it into English here, lest by chance it might be repeated too often and so give pain to good men; but scholars may read it.) But I have never known a brother of a friars' Order to take it as the text for a public sermon in English and expound it without gloss. They preach that penance is profitable for the soul, and speak of the suffering and pain that Christ endured for men. But this fat-cheeked holy glutton has no compassion on us poor people,' I said to Patience, 'he behaves badly, failing to practise what he preaches.' Indeed, I heartily wished that the dishes and platters set before this doctor were become molten lead in his stomach, and the devil there along with them! 'I am going to argue this bottle-bellied chamber-pot into giving me a definition of that penance which he recently preached about.'

Patience perceived my thoughts and winked at me to be quiet, saying: 'In a minute, when his capacity is exhausted, you will see him doing his penance in his stomach, puffing at every word. His guts will rumble, and then he will yawn. He

And seyde, 'Þow shalt se þus sone, whan he may no more,
He shal haue a penaunce in his paunche and puffe at ech a worde,
And þanne shullen his guttis godele and he shal galpen after;
For now he hath dronken so depe he wil deuyne sone,
And preuen it by her Pocalips and passioun of seynt Auereys,   [70
Þat neither bacoun ne braune, blancmangere ne mortrewes,
Is noither fisshe ne flesshe, but fode for a penaunte.
And þanne shal he testifye of a trinitee and take his felawe to
                                                                                  witnesse,
What he fonde in a freyel after a freres lyuynge,
And but if þe fyrst lyne be lesyng, leue me neuere after!   [75
And þanne is tyme to take and to appose þis doctoure
Of Dowel and of Dobet, and if Dobest be any penaunce.'—
    And I sete stille, as Pacience seyde, and þus sone þis doctour,
As rody as a rose rubbed his chekes,
Coughed and carped, and Conscience hym herde,   [80
And tolde hym of a trinite and toward vs he loked.
'What is Dowel? sire doctour,' quod I, 'is Dowel any penaunce?'
'Dowel?' quod þis doctour—and toke þe cuppe and dranke—
'Do non yuel to þine euenecrystene nouȝt by þi powere.'
    'By þis day, sire doctour,' quod I, 'þanne be ȝe nouȝt in Dowel; [85
For ȝe han harmed vs two in þat ȝe eten þe puddyng,
Mortrewes, and other mete, and we no morsel hade!
And if ȝe fare so in ȝowre fermorie, ferly me þinketh,
But chest be þere charite shulde be, and ȝonge childern dorste
                                                                                  pleyne!
I wolde permute my penaunce with ȝowre for I am in poynte to
                                                                                  Dowel!' [90
    Þanne Conscience curteisliche a contenaunce he made,
And preynte vpon Pacience to preie me to be stille,
And seyde hymself: 'Sire doctour, and it be ȝowre wille,
What is Dowel and Dobet? ȝe deuynours knoweth.'
    'Dowel,' quod þis doctour; 'do as clerkes techeth,   [95
And Dobet is he þat techeth and trauailleth to teche other,
And Dobest doth hymself so as he seith and precheth:
        Qui facit et docuerit, magnus vocabitur in regno celorum.'
    'Now þow, Clergye,' quod Conscience, 'carpest what is Dowel.'
'I haue seuene sones,' he seyde, 'seruen in a castel,
Þere þe Lorde of lyf wonyeth, to leren hym what is Dowel;   [100
Til I se þo seuene and myself acorden,
I am vnhardy', quod he, 'to any wyȝt to preue it.

---

⁷¹ blancmangere: MS blanmangere or blaumangere   ⁸⁷ morsel: MS mussel

has drunk so much by now that he will promptly explain (proving his words by the Gluttons' Apocalypse and by the Passion of St Avoya) that bacon and brawn and rich pies and pâtés are neither fish nor meat, but suitable food for a penitent. Then he will testify by the Trinity, calling his companion to witness, what meagre food may be found in a friar's provision-basket, in accordance with his way of living. If his words are not a lie from the very start, never trust me again! Then will be the time to set to work questioning this doctor about Do Well and Do Better, and about whether Do Best is any form of penance.'

I sat still, as Patience told me to, and in a short time this rosy-faced doctor rubbed his cheeks and coughed and began to speak. Conscience, hearing him, mentioned a triple topic to him, and he looked in our direction.

'Reverend Doctor,' I said, 'what is Do Well? Is it some kind of penance?'

'Do Well?' said the doctor, picking up his cup and drinking from it. 'It is to do no wrong to your fellow Christian, so far as it lies in your power.'

'In that case, Doctor,' I said, 'you are certainly not practising Do Well, for you have done harm to both of us, since you ate the pudding and the pâtés and the other food, and we did not have a morsel. If this is the kind of treatment you apply in your infirmary, it seems remarkable to me if strife is not to be found there, where love ought to be—were the young boys to dare to complain! I am willing to exchange my penance for yours, for I am all set to Do Well.'

Then Conscience made a courteous gesture, glancing at Patience to ask me to be quiet, and said: 'If you please, Doctor, what are Do Well and Do Better? You expounders of the Scriptures have this knowledge.'

'Do Well', said the doctor, 'is to do as the clergy teach you. Do Better lies in teaching and striving hard in the instruction of others. Do Best lies in carrying out oneself what one says and preaches; "he who does and teaches [the commandments of God] shall be called great in the kingdom of heaven".'

'And now you, Learning,' said Conscience, 'tell us what Do Well is.'

He said: 'I have seven sons, who are servants in a castle where the Lord of Life dwells, to teach them what Do Well is. Until I find those seven and myself agreed, I lack confidence to define it to anyone, for a certain Piers the Ploughman has

For one Pieres þe Ploughman hath inpugned vs alle,
And sette alle sciences at a soppe, saue loue one,
And no tixte ne taketh to meyntene his cause,   [105
But *dilige deum* and *domine, quis habitabit, &c.*
And seith þat Dowel and Dobet aren two infinites,
Whiche infinites, with a feith, fynden oute Dobest,
Which shal saue mannes soule; þus seith Piers þe Ploughman.
   'I can nouȝt her-on', quod Conscience, 'ac I knowe wel Pieres;
                                                                 [110

He wil nouȝt aȝein holy writ speken, I dar wel vndertake;
Þanne passe we ouer til Piers come and preue þis in dede.
Pacience hath be in many place and perauntre cnoweth
Þat no clerke ne can, as Cryst bereth witnesse:
      Pacientes vincunt, &c.'
'At ȝowre preyere,' quod Pacyence þo, 'so no man displese hym;
                                                                 [115

Disce,' quod he, '*doce, dilige inimicos.*
Disce, and Dowel; *doce*, and Dobet;
Dilige, and Dobest; þus tauȝte me ones
A lemman þat I loued, Loue was hir name.
"With wordes and with werkes", quod she, "and wille of þyne
                                                        herte, [120

Þow loue lelly þi soule al þi lyf-tyme;
And so þow lere þe to louye, for þe Lordes loue of heuene,
Þine enemye in al wyse euene-forth with þiselue.
Cast coles on his hed, and al kynde speche,
Bothe with werkes and with wordes fonde his loue to wynne,   [125
And lay on hym þus with loue til he laughe on þe;
And but he bowe for þis betyng, blynde mote he worthe!"'. . . .

   'It is but a Dido', quod þis doctour, 'a dysoures tale.
Al þe witt of þis worlde and wiȝte mennes strengthe
Can nouȝt confourmen a pees bytwene þe pope and his enemys,
                                                                 [130

Ne bitwene two Cristene kynges can no wiȝte pees make
Profitable to ayther peple'; and put þe table fro hym,
And toke Clergye and Conscience to conseille, as it were,
Þat Pacience þo moste passe, for pilgrimes kunne wel lye.
   Ac Conscience carped loude and curteislich seide,   [135
'Frendes, fareth wel!' and faire spake to Clergye,
'For I wil go with þis gome, if God wil ȝiue me grace,

---

126 laughe: ms laghe

called us all in question, setting no store by any form of knowledge, save love alone. The only texts he uses to uphold his cause are "Love God!" and "O Lord, who shall sojourn [in thy tent]?" and so on. He says that Do Well and Do Better are two terms lacking positive definition, which, when coupled with faith, find their realisation in Do Best, which will save man's soul. This is the verdict of Piers the Plough-man.'

'I am ignorant in these matters,' said Conscience, 'but I know Piers well and am ready to vouch for it that he will not say anything that is contrary to Holy Scripture. So let us pass over the matter until Piers shall come and demonstrate the answer in practice. Patience has been in many places; perhaps he knows what learned men do not know, since, as Christ testifies, "the patient conquer".'

Then Patience said: 'If you wish, provided that it causes no offence to anyone. *Learn; teach; love your enemies!* By learning, you Do Well; by teaching, you Do Better; by loving, you Do Best. A friend whom I loved dearly, whose name was Love, once taught me thus, saying: "All your life, cherish your soul faithfully in word and deed and intention, and so, for love of the heavenly Lord, teach yourself to love your enemy as yourself in every way. Cast coals of fire on his head by kindness of speech, strive to gain his love by your deeds and your words, and belabour him with love until he smiles at you. If such chastisement does not bring him to his knees, he deserves to lose his sight".'

'This is old stuff, known to every spinner of tales', said the doctor. 'All the wisdom in the world and strong men's vigour are powerless to achieve peace between the Pope and his enemies, and no one can make a peace treaty between two Christian kings which will profit both nations.' With that, he pushed the table aside, and held a conference with Learning and Conscience, advising that Patience should be made to leave, since pilgrims are ready liars.

However, Conscience spoke up, and said politely: 'Fare well, my friends', adding courteously to Learning: 'If God will grant me grace, I will go on pilgrimage with Patience until I have acquired more experience.'

Learning said to Conscience: 'Do you mean to say that you

And be pilgryme with Pacience til I haue proued more.'
'What?' quod Clergye to Conscience, 'ar ȝe coueitouse nouthe
After ȝeresȝyues or ȝiftes, or ȝernen to rede redeles?   [140
I shal brynge ȝow a bible, a boke of þe olde lawe,
And lere ȝow, if ȝow lyke, þe leest poynte to knowe,
Þat Pacience þe pilgryme perfitly knewe neuere.'
    'Nay, bi Cryste,' quod Conscience to Clergye, 'God þe forȝelde,
For al þat Pacience me profreth proude am I litel.   [145
Ac þe wille of þe wye and þe wille of folke here
Hath moeued my mode to mourne for my synnes.
Þe good wille of a wiȝte was neure bouȝte to þe fulle;
For þere nys no tresore þerto to a trewe wille.
Haued nouȝt Magdeleigne more for a boxe of salue,   [150
Þan Zacheus for he seide *dimidium bonorum meorum do pauperibus*?
And þe pore widwe for a peire of mytes,
Þan alle þo that offreden into *gazafiliacium*?'
Þus curteislich Conscience congeyde fyrst þe frere,
And sithen softliche he seyde in Clergyes ere,   [155
'Me were leuer, by owre Lorde, and I lyue shulde,
Haue pacience perfitlich þan half þi pakke of bokes!'
Clergye to Conscience no congeye wolde take,
But seide ful sobreliche: 'þow shalt se þe tyme,
Whan þow art wery for-walked, wilne me to consaille.'   [160
    'Þat is soth,' seyde Conscience, 'so me God helpe!
If Pacience be owre partyng felawe and pryue with vs bothe,
There nys wo in þis worlde þat we ne shulde amende,
And confourmen kynges to pees, and al kynnes londes,
Sarasenes and Surre, and so forth alle þe Iewes   [165
Turne into þe trewe feithe and intil one byleue.'
    'Þat is soth,' quod Clergye, 'I se what þow menest,
I shal dwelle as I do my deuore to shewen,
And conformen fauntekynes and other folke ylered,
Tyl Pacience haue preued þe and parfite þe maked.'   [170
    Conscience þo with Pacience passed, pilgrymes as it were.
Þanne had Pacience, as pylgrymes han, in his poke vittailles,
Sobrete, and symple-speche and sothfaste-byleue,
To conforte hym and Conscience if þey come in place
Þere Vnkyndenesse and Coueytise is, hungrye contrees bothe.   [175
    And as þei went by þe weye, of Dowel þei carped;
Þei mette with a mynstral, as me þo þouȝte.
Pacience apposed hym fyrste and preyed hym he sholde hem telle

---

146 of folke: of *supplied*

are now seeking New Year gifts or presents, or do you desire to find the answer to riddles? If that is your wish, I will bring you one of the books of the Old Testament and teach you to understand every minute detail—such things as Patience the pilgrim never fully comprehended.'

'God bless you, no!' Conscience told him. 'I take no pride in anything that Patience offers me, but his intent and the intent of those here have prompted my mind to sorrow for my sins. A man's good intent can never be adequately paid for, because no treasure can stand comparison with an honest intent. Did not Mary Magdalen receive more in return for a box of ointment than Zacchaeus did for saying "the half of my goods I give to the poor", or the poor widow for two copper coins than all those who put their gifts into the treasury?'

So Conscience first courteously took his leave of the friar, and then murmured in an aside to Learning: 'If my life be spared, our Lord knows I would rather have perfect patience than half your bundle of books!' Learning refused to bid Conscience farewell, saying, with deep seriousness: 'The time will come when you are worn out with walking and desire my advice.'

'That is true, God help me!' said Conscience. 'If we may share the companionship of Patience, and if he may be the intimate friend of us both, there is no trouble in the world that we could not put right. We could establish peace between kings and between all nations, and convert the Saracens and the Syrians and, finally, all the Jews to the true faith and to one creed.'

'True,' said Learning, 'I see what you mean. I shall continue to do my duty in my present fashion, establishing children, and those under instruction, in the faith, until Patience has put you to the test and made you perfect.'

Then Conscience and Patience went on their way in pilgrims' fashion. Patience, as pilgrims do, carried provisions in his pouch—temperance, simplicity of speech and steadfast faith—to keep up the strength of Conscience and himself if they chanced to enter the hungry lands where uncharitableness and covetousness are to be found.

As they went along, talking about Do Well, they met a man who appeared to be a minstrel. Patience questioned him first, asking him to tell Conscience and himself what trade he followed and where he was going.

To Conscience, what crafte he couthe an to what contree he wolde.
   'I am a mynstral,' quod þat man, 'my name is *Actiua-vita*:   [180
Alle ydel ich hatye, for of actyf is my name.
A wafrere, wil ȝe wite, and serue many lordes,
And fewe robes I fonge or furred gounes.
Couthe I lye to do men laughe, þanne lacchen I shulde
Other mantel or money amonges lordes mynstralles.   [185
Ac for I can noither tabre ne trompe ne telle none gestes,
Farten, ne fythelen at festes, ne harpen,
Iape ne iogly ne gentlych pype,
Ne noyther sailly ne saute ne synge with þe gyterne,
I haue none gode gyftes of þise grete lordes,   [190
For no bred þat I brynge forth, saue a beneson on þe Sonday,
Whan þe prest preyeth þe peple her *pater-noster* to bidde
For Peres þe Plowman and þat hym profite wayten.
And þat am I, Actyf, þat ydelnesse hatye,
For alle trewe trauaillours and tilieres of þe erthe;   [195
Fro Mychelmesse to Mychelmesse I fynde hem with wafres.
   Beggeres and bidderes of my bred crauen,
Faitoures and freres and folke with brode crounes.
I fynde payne for þe pope and prouendre for his palfrey,
And I hadde neuere of hym, haue God my treuthe,   [200
Noither prouendre ne parsonage ȝut of þe popis ȝifte,
Saue a pardoun with a peys of led and two pollis amydde!
Hadde iche a clerke þat couthe write, I wolde caste hym a bille,
Þat he sent me vnder his seel a salue for þe pestilence,
And þat his blessyng and his bulles bocches miȝte destroye: [205
      In nomine meo demonia eicient, et super egros manus imponent, et
                                             bene habebunt.

And þanne wolde I be prest to þe peple paste for to make,
And buxome and busy aboute bred and drynke
For hym and for alle his, fonde I þat his pardoun
Miȝte lechen a man as I bileue it shulde.
For sith he hath þe powere þat Peter hymself hadde,   [210
He hath þe potte with þe salue sothly, as me þinketh:
      Argentum et aurum non est mihi; quod autem habeo, hoc tibi do; in
                                             nomine domini, surge et ambula.

Ac if miȝte of miracle hym faille, it is for men ben nouȝt worthy
To haue þe grace of God, and no gylte of þe pope.
For may no blyssyng done vs bote but if we wil amende,
Ne mannes masse make pees amonges Cristene peple,   [215

---

206 *eicient*: MS *eiciunt*   206 *þe supplied*   211 *hoc supplied*

The man said: 'I am a minstrel; my name is Active Life.
Since I am called "active", I loathe all idle people. If you wish
to know, I am a maker of wafer-bread and supply many
lords, but I receive little in the way of fine garments or fur-
trimmed gowns. If I knew how to make people laugh by
inventing stories, then I should come by either clothes or
cash, along with the lords' minstrels; but since I can play
neither the drum nor the trumpet, nor tell anecdotes or make
vulgar noises, nor play the fiddle or the harp at banquets,
clown, juggle, play sweet music on the pipes, leap, jump, or
sing to the guitar, I get no fine presents from these great
lords, whatever bread I provide. My only reward is a blessing
on Sundays, when the priest asks the people to say an Our
Father for Piers the Ploughman and those who further his
profits. Such a one am I, the Active Man, with my hatred of
idleness. From one Michaelmas to the next, I provide wafers
for all honest labourers and tillers of the soil. Beggars and
mendicants desire my bread, and so do vagabonds and friars and
those who wear the tonsure. I provide bread for the Pope and
fodder for his horse, but I swear to God that I never yet re-
ceived a prebendary's stall or a parsonage at the Pope's hand—
only a Pardon with a lead seal, bearing the impression of the
heads of St Peter and St Paul. If I had a scribe who could write
for me, I would devise a petition to him, asking that he should
send me, under his seal, a remedy for the plague, and that his
blessing and his bulls should have the power to cure swellings,
since Christ said: "In my name they will cast out demons;
they will lay hands on the sick, and they will recover". I
would then be prompt to make pastry for the people, and set
to work readily to find bread and drink for him and his fol-
lowers, if I found that his Pardon could heal people, as I
think it should; for since he has the power that St Peter
himself had, it seems to me that he must have the jar of
healing ointment. "I have no silver and gold," said Peter, "but
I give you what I have; in the name of Jesus Christ of Nazareth,
walk." However, if the Pope lacks the power to work
miracles, it is through no fault of his own, but because men
are not worthy to receive the grace of God; for no blessing
can cure us unless we are willing to mend our ways, and no
Mass can make peace between Christians until pride is utterly
destroyed—and that must be through lack of bread.

Tyl pruyde be purelich fordo, and þat þourgh payn defaute.
  For ar I haue bred of mele, ofte mote I swete.
And ar þe comune haue corne ynough many a colde mornynge;
So, ar my wafres ben ywrouȝt, moche wo I tholye.
  Alle Londoun I leue liketh wel my wafres,   [220
And lowren whan þei lakken hem—it is nouȝt longe ypassed,
Þere was a carful comune whan no carte come to toune
With bake bred fro Stretforth; þo gan beggeres wepe,
And werkmen were agaste a litel, þis wil be þouȝte longe.
In þe date of owre dryȝte, in a drye Apprile,   [225
A þousande and thre hondreth tweis thretty and ten,
My wafres þere were gesen, whan Chichestre was maire.'
  I toke gode kepe, by Cryst and Conscience bothe,
Of Haukyn þe actyf man and how he was y-clothed.
He hadde a cote of Crystendome, as holykirke bileueth,   [230
Ac it was moled in many places with many sondri plottes,
Of pruyde here a plotte, and þere a plotte of vnboxome speche,
Of scornyng and of scoffyng and of vnskilful berynge,
As in aparaille and in porte proude amonges þe peple,
Otherwyse þan he hath with herte or syȝte shewynge;   [235
Hym willynge þat alle men wende he were þat he is nouȝte.
For-why he bosteth and braggeth with many bolde othes,
And inobedient to ben vndernome of any lyf lyuynge,
And so syngulere by hymself as to syȝte of þe poeple,
Was none suche as hymself, ne none so pope-holy,   [240
Y-habited as an hermyte, an ordre by hym-selue,
Religioun sanz reule and resonable obedience;
Lakkyng lettred men and lewed men bothe,
In lykyng of lele lyf and a lyer in soule;
With inwit and with outwitt ymagenen and studye,   [245
As best for his body be to haue a badde name,
And entermeten hym oueral þer he hath nouȝt to done,
Wilnyng þat men wende his witte were þe best.
And if he gyueth ouȝte pore gomes, telle what he deleth;
Pore of possessioun in purse and in coffre,   [250
And as a lyon on to loke and lordeliche of speche.
Baldest of beggeres, a bostour þat nouȝt hath,
In towne and in tauernes tales to telle,
And segge þinge þat he neuere seigh and for soth sweren it;
Of dedes þat he neuere dyd, demen and bosten,   [255
And of werkes þat he wel dyd witnesse and seggen:

²²¹ hem: MS it   ²²³ bake *supplied*   ²⁴⁰ pope: MS pompe

'On many a cold morning, I have to sweat to get meal before I can make bread, and before enough grain can be found for the people; so I suffer a great deal of hardship before my wafers are made.

'All Londoners, I think, enjoy my wafers and are out of temper when they cannot get them. It is not so long since the public were full of worry, at the time when no carts were coming into town from Stratford with bread. Beggars wept, and workmen were pretty scared, as will be remembered for a long time.—During the dry April of the year of our Lord 1370, when Chichester was Mayor: that was when my wafers were scarce.'

Conscience and I both took good heed of Haukyn the Active Man and of the state of his clothes. His coat was made of the Christian faith professed by Holy Church, but it was badly soiled with many different stains. It was blotched with pride in one place, in another with rebellious speech, with scornfulness and scoffing and outrageous behaviour, showing arrogance towards others in his dress and in his manner, with inward or outward dissembling, wanting everyone to think him to be something other than he really was. Therefore he was a boaster and a braggart, given to much bold swearing, accepting criticism from no man alive. He appeared to the world to be in a class by himself; there was no one quite like him, no one so full of feigned holiness. He was garbed like a hermit belonging to an Order all of his own, a Religious lacking both rule and proper obedience. He found fault with the educated and the ignorant alike. He wished to seem an honest-man, but he was a liar at heart. He devoted his faculties and senses to studiously devising what would be best for his body, to the detriment of his good name. He constantly meddled in matters that did not concern him. He wished to be thought superior to all in intellect. If he gave anything to the poor, he made public the amount of his gift. The contents of his purse and his coffer were meagre, but he had the air of a lion and talked like a lord. He was a thoroughly unabashed beggar, a boaster without a penny, who spun tales in the town and the taverns, speaking of things he never saw and swearing that they were true, airing his views on deeds he never performed, and boasting about them, and bearing witness to his own good actions, saying: 'See, now! If you do

'Lo! if ȝe leue me nouȝt, or þat I lye wenen,
Axeth at hym or at hym, and he ȝow can telle,
What I suffred and seighe and sometymes hadde,
And what I couth and knewe, and what kynne I come of.'   [260
Al he wolde þat men wiste, of werkes and of wordes,
Which myȝte plese þe peple and praysen hymseluen:

> Si hominibus placerem, Christi seruus non essem;
> Et alibi: nemo potest duobus dominis seruire.

'Bi Criste,' quod Conscience þo, 'þi best cote, Haukyn,
Hath many moles and spottes; it moste ben ywasshe.'
'Ȝe, whoso toke hede,' quod Haukyn, 'byhynde and bifore,   [265
What on bakke and what on bodyhalf and by þe two sydes,
Men sholde fynde many frounces and many foule plottes.'

And he torned hym as tyte and þanne toke I hede,
It was fouler by felefolde þan it firste semed.
It was bidropped with wratthe and wikked wille,   [270
With enuye and yuel speche, entysyng to fyȝte,
Lyinge and laughynge and leue tonge to chyde;
Al þat he wist wykked by any wiȝte, tellen it,
And blame men bihynde her bakke and bydden hem meschaunce;
And þat he wist bi Wille, tellen it Watte,   [275
And þat Watte wiste, Wille wiste it after,
And made of frendes foes þorugh a false tongue,
'Or with myȝte of mouthe or þorugh mannes strengthe
Auenge me fele tymes, other frete myselue
Wythinne, as a shepster shere; '—i-shrewed men and cursed!   [280

> Cuius ma勝勝勝勝ma勝ma勝勝maledic勝cione os plenum est, et amaritudine; sub lingua eius
> labor et dolor:
> Et alibi: filij hominum, dentes eorum arma et sagitte, et lingua
> eorum gladius acutus:—

'Þere is no lyf þat I louye lastyng any while,
For tales þat I telle no man trusteth to me,
And whan I may nouȝt haue þe maistrye, with malencolye I take,
Þat I cacche þe crompe, þe cardiacle some tyme,
Or an ague in suche an angre, and some tyme a feure,   [285
Þat taketh me al a twelf-moneth, tyl þat I dispyse
Lechecrafte of owre Lorde, and leue on a wicche,
And segge þat no clerke ne can, ne Cryste, as I leue,
To þe souter of Southwerke, or of Shordyche dame Emme!
And segge þat no Goddes worde gaf me neuere bote,   [290
But þorw a charme had I chaunce and my chief hele!'

287 of: MS or

not believe me, or think that I am lying, ask such-a-one, or such-a-one. He will be able to tell you what I have suffered and seen, and what possessions I once had, and what ability and knowledge, and who my family were.' He was bent on having people know of actions and sayings likely to win public approval and bring credit on himself. ('If I were still pleasing men, I should not be a servant of Christ', says St Paul; and the Gospel: 'No one can serve two masters'.)

Then Conscience said: 'By Christ, Haukyn, your best coat is badly stained and splashed. It needs washing.'

'Yes,' said Haukyn, 'if anyone looked hard all over, they would find many creases and filthy marks on the back and the front and on both sides.'

He turned round quickly, and then I noticed that it was far dirtier than it seemed at first. It was bespattered with anger and ill will, with envy and malicious speech, the inducing of quarrels, lies, and mockery, and a tongue quick to scold. He would pass on all the evil that he knew of anyone, and criticise people behind their backs and wish them misfortune. He would repeat to Walter what he knew about Will, and what Walter knew, Will subsequently learned. He turned friends into enemies by his lying tongue. 'Time and again', he said, 'I avenge myself, either by force of speech or by strong-armed men; otherwise I inwardly jag myself like a cutter's scissors.' Such men are wretched and accursed. [As one Psalm says:] 'His mouth is filled with cursing and deceit and oppression; under his tongue are mischief and iniquity'; and another speaks of 'the sons of men, whose teeth are spears and arrows, and their tongue a sharp sword'.

'I love no one for any length of time; no one trusts me, because of the tales I tell. When I cannot have the upper hand, I become afflicted with melancholic bile, so that I develop cramp or cardiac pain on occasion, or ague, through my distress, and sometimes a fever that grips me for a full twelve months, until I come to despise our Lord's skill as a doctor and put my trust in witches, and say that no learned priest, nor even Christ Himself, can, to my mind, compare in ability with the cobbler of Southwark or Dame Emma of Shoreditch. I say, too, that none of God's words ever cured me, but that it was a charm that brought me luck and most relief.'

I wayted wisloker, and þanne was it soiled
With lykyng of lecherye, as by lokyng of his eye.
For vche a mayde þat he mette, he made hir a signe
Semynge to-synne-ward, and some tyme he gan taste   [295
Aboute þe mouth, or bynethe bygynneth to grope,
Tyl eytheres wille waxeth kene and to þe werke ȝeden,
As wel in fastyng-days and Frydayes and forboden nyȝtes;
And as wel in Lente as oute of Lente, alle tymes ylyche,
Suche werkes with hem were neuere oute of sesoun,   [300
Tyl þei myȝte namore; and þanne had merye tales,
And how þat lechoures louyen lauȝen an iapen,
And of her harlotrye and horedome in her elde tellen.
    Thanne Pacience parceyued of poyntes of his cote,
Was colmy þorw coueityse and vnkynde desyrynge;   [305
More to good þan to God þe gome his loue caste,
And ymagyned how he it myȝte haue
With false mesures and mette and with false witnesse;
Lened for loue of þe wedde, and loth to do treuthe,
And awaited þorwgh which wey to bigile,   [310
And menged his marchaundyse and made a gode moustre:
'Þe worste within was; a gret witte I lete hit,
And if my neighbore had any hyne, or any beste elles,
More profitable þan myne, many sleightes I made,
How I myȝte haue it al my witte I caste,   [315
And but I it had by other waye atte laste I stale it,
Or pryuiliche his purse shoke, vnpiked his lokkes,
Or by nyȝt or by day aboute was ich euere
Þorwgh gyle to gadren þe good þat ich haue.
Ȝif I ȝede to þe plow, I pynched so narwe   [320
Þat a fote-londe or a forwe fecchen I wolde,
Of my nexte neighbore nymen of his erthe;
And if I rope, ouer-reche, or ȝaf hem red þat ropen,
To seise to me with her sykel þat I ne sewe neure.
And whoso borwed of me abouȝte þe tyme   [325
With presentes priueliche, or payed somme certeyne.
So, walde he or nouȝt wolde he, wynnen I wolde;
And bothe to kyth and to kyn vnkynde of þat ich hadde.
And whoso cheped my chaffare chiden I wolde,
But he profred to paye a peny or tweyne   [330
More þan it was worth, and ȝet wolde I swere

---

300 were: MS was   304 of his: of *supplied*   305 vnkynde: MS vkynde
323 I *supplied*   325 borwed: MS borweth; abouȝte: MS aboute

When I examined his coat more closely, it was soiled with lecherous desire, to be seen in the glance of his eye. To every girl he met he made a gesture inciting her to sin, and sometimes he kissed her on the mouth, or began to pass his hands under her clothes, until desire grew keen in both of them and they proceeded to the act of love, even on fast-days and Fridays and prohibited nights, in Lent as well as out of Lent; all times were alike. For them, such acts were never out of season. When at last they grew impotent, they exchanged lewd stories, laughing and joking about how lechers enjoy themselves, recalling, in their old age, their profligacy and loose living.

Then Patience noticed how his coat was begrimed in some places with covetousness and more than natural desire for possessions. The man set his heart on goods rather than on God, and figured out how he could obtain them by false weights and measures and by false declarations. He lent money because he had his eye on the pledge; he had no fancy for honest dealing and was on the look-out for ways of cheating. He made a good display of his wares by mixing them up together. 'The worst were concealed within', he said. 'I thought this was a fine idea. If a neighbour of mine had a more valuable servant or beast than I had, I devised many schemes and turned my mind wholly to ways of obtaining it, and if I could not get it by any other means, I finally stole it; or I would surreptitiously empty out his purse, or pick his locks, or busy myself night and day in gathering together by fraud the wealth which I possess. If I went ploughing, I would squeeze so close to the land of the neighbour nearest to me that I stole a foot or a furrow of it from him. If I went reaping, I, or my reapers acting on my instructions, would reach over and use their sickles to steal, for my benefit, the crop that was never sown by me.

'Anyone who borrowed from me had to purchase time either by secret gifts or by the payment of a fixed sum, so that, whether he liked it or not, I was the gainer. Furthermore, I ignored the natural claims of my relations on me. I heaped abuse on anyone who bargained for my wares unless he agreed to pay a penny or two more than they were worth, and even then I would swear, with many oaths, that they had

G

Þat it coste me moche more, swore many othes.
  In halydayes at holicherche whan ich herde masse
Hadde I neuere wille, wot God, witterly to biseche
Mercye for my mysdedes, þat I ne morned more   [335
For losse of gode, leue me, þan for my lykames giltes;
As, if I had dedly synne done, I dred nouȝt þat so sore
As when I lened and leued it lost, or longe ar it were payed.
So if I kydde any kyndenesse myn euen-Cristene to helpe,
Vpon a cruel coueityse myn herte gan hange.   [340
And if I sent ouer see my seruantz to Bruges,
Or into Pruslonde my prentys, my profit to wayten,
To marchaunden with monoye and maken her eschaunges,
Miȝte neuere me conforte in þe mene tyme
Noither messe ne matynes, ne none manere siȝtes,   [345
Ne neuere penaunce perfourned, ne *pater-noster* seyde,
Þat my mynde ne was more on my gode, in a doute,
Þan in þe grace of God and his grete helpes:
    Vbi thesaurus tuus, ibi et cor tuum.' . . . .

  Thus Haukyn þe actyf man hadde ysoiled his cote,
Til Conscience acouped hym þereof in a curteise manere [350
Whi he ne hadde wasshen it or wyped it with a brusshe.
  'I haue but one hool hatere,' quod Haukyn, 'I am þe lasse to
                                                      blame
Þough it be soiled and selde clene; I slepe þereinne on niȝtes;
And also I haue an houswyf, hewen and children—
    vxorem duxy, et ideo non possum venire—
Þat wolen bymolen it many tyme, maugre my chekes!   [355
It hath ben laued in lente and oute of lente bothe
With þe sope of sykenesse, þat seketh wonder depe,
And with þe losse of catel; loth forto agulte
God or any gode man, bi auȝte þat I wiste,
And was shryuen of þe preste þat gaue me, for my synnes, [360
To penaunce, pacyence, and pore men to fede,
Al for coueitise of my Crystenedome in clennesse to kepen it.
And couthe I neuere, by Cryste, kepen it clene an houre
Þat I ne soiled it with syȝte or sum ydel speche,
Or þorugh werke or þorugh worde or wille of myn herte, [365
Þat I ne flober it foule fro morwe tyl eue.'
  'And I shal kenne þe', quod Conscience, 'of contricioun to make,

cost me much more. When I heard Mass in church on holy days, God knows indeed I was never minded to pray for mercy on account of my sins without sorrowing more, I assure you, for the loss of my goods than for the sins of my flesh. For example, I was far less afraid when I had committed mortal sin than when I had lent money and thought that it was lost or that its repayment was long delayed. If I showed any natural kindly disposition to help my fellow Christians, my heart promptly fastened on uncharitable avarice. If I sent my servants across the sea to Bruges, or my apprentice into Prussia, to keep an eye on my profits, to trade with money and to barter, neither Mass nor Mattins, nor anything I beheld, nor the doing of penance nor the saying of Paternosters could comfort me during the time they were away, or prevent my mind from dwelling with fear on my goods, rather than on the grace and the mighty succour of God: "where your treasure is, there will your heart be also".'

In this manner Haukyn the Active Man had soiled his coat, until Conscience found fault with him courteously, asking why he had failed to wash or brush it.

Haukyn said: 'I have only the one sound garment. I am the less to blame if it is soiled and rarely clean. I sleep with it wrapped round me at night, and then, too, I have a wife and servants and children who constantly dirty it, no matter what I do. [Like the man in the parable,] "I have married a wife, and therefore I cannot come." Both in Lent and out of Lent it has been washed with the penetrating soap of illness and with the loss of my goods. I have been anxious not to offend against God or good men knowingly in anything. I have confessed to the priest, who gave me, as penance for my sins, patience, and the feeding of the poor, and bade me, as I prized my baptism, to keep my coat unsullied. Yet, God knows, I could never keep it clean for an hour without soiling it through sight, or foolish talk, or deed or word or desire, nor avoid muddying it with filth from morning to night.'

'I will teach you to achieve contrition,' said Conscience,

Þat shal clawe þi cote of alkynnes filthe,
>   *Cordis contricio, etc.;*
Dowel shal wasshen it and wryngen it þorw a wys confessour,
>   *Oris confessio, etc.;*
Dobet shal beten it and bouken it as briȝte as any scarlet,   [370
And engreynen it with good wille and Goddes grace to amende þe,
And sithen sende þe to satisfaccioun for to sowen it after,
>   *Satisfaccio dobest.*
Shal neuere myste bimolen it, ne moth after biten it,
Ne fende ne false man defoulen it in þi lyue;
Shall none heraude ne harpoure haue a fairere garnement   [375
Þan Haukyn þe actyf man, and þow do by my techyng;
Ne no mynstral be more worth, amonges pore and riche,
Þan Haukynnes wyf þe wafrere, with his *actiua-vita.*'
    'And I shal purueye þe paste,' quod Pacyence, 'þough no plow
>   erie,
And floure to fede folke with, as best be for þe soule,   [380
Þough neuere greyne growed, ne grape vppon vyne.
Alle þat lyueth and loketh lyflode wolde I fynde,
And þat ynough shal none faille of þinge þat hem nedeth.
We shulde nouȝt be to busy abouten owre lyflode,
>   *Ne solliciti sitis, etc.: volucres celi deus pascit, etc.: pacientes*
>   *vincunt, etc.*'

    Þanne laughed Haukyn a litel, and liȝtly gan swerye,   [385
'Who so leueth ȝow, by owre Lorde, I leue nouȝte he be blissed!'
'No', quod Pacyence paciently, and out of his poke hente
Vitailles of grete vertues for al manere bestes,
And seyde, 'Lo! here lyflode ynough, if owre byleue be trewe!
For lente neuere was lyf but lyflode were shapen,   [390
Wherof or wherfore or whereby to lybbe.
    Firste þe wylde worme vnder weet erthe,
Fissch to lyue in þe flode and in þe fyre þe crykat,
Þe corlue by kynde of þe eyre, moste clennest flesch of bryddes,
And bestes by grasse and by greyne and by grene rotis,   [395
In menynge þat alle men myȝte þe same
Lyue þorw lele byleue and loue, as God witnesseth;
>   *Quodcumque pecieritis a patre in nomine meo, &c.: et alibi,*
>   *Non in solo pane viuit homo, set in omni verbo quod procedit de*
>   *ore dei.*'

But I loked what lyflode it was þat Pacience so preysed,
And þanne was it a pece of þe *pater-noster, fiat voluntas tua.*

369 shal *supplied*

' "contrition of heart", that will scrape your coat entirely free
of filth. Do Well will wash and wring it by means of a wise
confessor—that is, through "confession with the mouth". Do
Better will pummel it and steep it in cleansing fluid until it
glows like scarlet, and fast dye it with good desires and the
grace of God to bring you to amendment, and then send you
to the making of satisfaction through penance—"satisfaction
of deed", which is Do Best—to sew it up again.

'From then on, while you live, fog will never befoul it, nor
moth devour it, nor devil or false men defile it. No herald or
harper will have a brighter garment than Haukyn the Active
Man, if you act according to my teaching, and no minstrel will
receive more honour amongst rich and poor than the wife of
Haukyn the wafer-maker with his Active Life.'

'And I', said Patience, 'will provide you with dough, even
if no plough drives a furrow, and with flour to feed people as
is best for their souls, even if no grain grows, and no grapes on
the vine. I will find the means of life for all living beings, and
see that none go short of what they need. We should not
concern ourselves too busily about our livelihood: "Do not be
anxious about life, [what you shall eat, or what you shall
drink]; . . . Look at the birds of the air; . . . your heavenly
Father feeds them"; and also: "the patient conquer".'

Then Haukyn gave a short laugh and protested lightly: 'By
the Lord, I cannot think that anyone who puts his trust in
you will find many blessings!'

'On the contrary', said Patience patiently, and took from his
bag provisions full of nourishment for all manner of creatures.
He went on: 'If our faith is true, then here is sufficient liveli-
hood. For no life was ever given without the means of
livelihood being provided, by which life might be sustained.

'First, there is the worm in its freedom beneath the dank
earth; fish living in the streams, and the cricket on the hearth;
the curlew, purest-fleshed of all birds, living by nature on air,
and cattle on grass and grain and green roots, as a token that
every man might likewise live by unwavering faith and love,
as God has declared: "Whatever you ask in my name, I will
do it [that the Father may be glorified in the Son]", and also:
"Man shall not live by bread alone, but by every word that
proceeds from the mouth of God".'

I looked to see what this means of livelihood was that
Patience praised so highly and found it to be part of the Lord's
Prayer: "Thy will be done".

'Haue, Haukyn!' quod Pacyence, 'and ete þis whan þe hungreth,
[400

Or whan þow clomsest for colde, or clyngest for drye.
Shal neuere gyues þe greue, ne grete lordes wrath,
Prisone ne peyne, for *pacientes vincunt*.'. . .

Ac after my wakyng, it was wonder longe
Ar I couth kyndely knowe what was Dowel.   [405
And so my witte wex and wanyed til I a fole were,
And somme lakked my lyf, allowed it fewe,
And leten me for a lorel and loth to reuerencen
Lordes or ladyes or any lyf elles,
As persones in pellure, with pendauntes of syluer;   [410
To seriauntz, ne to suche, seyde nouȝte ones
'God loke ȝow, lordes!' ne louted faire;
þat folke helden me a fole, and in þat folye I raued,
Tyl Resoun hadde reuthe on me and rokked me aslepe,
Tyl I seigh, as it sorcerye were, a sotyl þinge withal, [415
One withouten tonge and teeth tolde me whyder I shulde,
And wherof I cam, and of what kynde; I coniured hym atte laste,
If he were Crystes creature, for Crystes loue me to tellen.
'I am Crystes creature', quod he, 'and Crystene in many a place,
In Crystes courte i-knowe wel, and of his kynne a partye. [420
Is noyther Peter þe porter, ne Poule with his fauchone,
þat wil defende me þe dore, dynge ich neure so late.
At mydnyȝt, at mydday, my voice so is y-knowe
þat eche a creature of his courte welcometh me fayre.'
'What ar ȝe called', quod I, 'in þat courte, amonges Crystes
                                        peple?' [425
'þe whiles I quykke þe corps', quod he, 'called am I *Anima*;
And whan I wilne and wolde, *Animus* ich hatte;
And for þat I can and knowe, called am I *Mens*;
And whan I make mone to God, *Memoria* is my name;
And whan I deme domes, and do as treuthe techeth,   [430
þanne is *Racio* my riȝt name, Resoun an Englisshe;
And whan I fele þat folke telleth, my firste name is *Sensus*,
And þat is wytte and wisdome, þe welle of alle craftes;
And whan I chalange or chalange nouȝte, chepe or refuse,
þanne am I Conscience y-calde, Goddis clerke and his notarie; [435
And whan I loue lelly owre Lorde and alle other,
þanne is lele Loue my name, and in Latyn *Amor*;

---

422 þat: MS þa

'Take this, Haukyn,' said Patience, 'and eat it when you are hungry, or numb with cold, or parched with thirst. Neither fetters, nor the wrath of potentates, nor prison, nor torment, will ever cause you distress, for "the patient conquer".'

After I awoke, many years passed before I could know in my heart what Do Well signified. My powers of understanding alternately grew and dwindled, until I became crazed. Some people censured my way of life; few praised it. I was considered a lazy wastrel, unwilling to show respect to lords or ladies or to anybody else, such as fur-clad priests with silver pendants on their belts. I never once said 'God save you, gentlemen!' to officers of the law and their like, or made them a polite bow. So people took me for a lunatic, and I raved in my lunacy until Reason took pity on me and rocked me to sleep. Then, as if by magic, I saw an uncanny sight: a tongueless, toothless being who told me whither I was bound and whence I came and of what nature I was. In the end I begged him to tell me, for the love of Christ, whether he was one of Christ's creatures.

'I *am* Christ's creature', he said, 'and a Christian to be found in many places. I am well known in Christ's court and am one of His family. Neither Peter, who keeps the gate, nor Paul with his sword, will bar the door against me, no matter how late I knock. My voice is so well known that every member of His court welcomes me warmly, whether it be noon or midnight.'

'By what name are you known among Christ's people in that court?' I asked.

'While I give life to the body, I am called "the living Soul" ,' he said. 'When my function is to wish or desire, I am called "Will". Inasmuch as I have knowledge and understanding, I am called "Mind". When I utter my complaint to God, my name is "Memory". When I make judgments and act according to the teaching of Truth, then my proper name is "Reason". When I observe what people say, my primary name is "Sense", that is to say, the wit and wisdom which are the source of all skills. When I claim or make no claim, buy or refuse to buy, then I am called "Conscience", God's clerk and scribe. When I faithfully love our Lord and all men, then my name is "True Love". When I take my flight from the body

And whan I flye fro þe flesshe and forsake þe caroigne,
Þanne am I spirit specheles and *Spiritus* þanne ich hatte.
Austyn and Ysodorus, ayther of hem bothe   [440
Nempned me þus to name; now þow myȝte chese
How þow coueitest to calle me, now þow knowest alle my
                                                                  names.'. . .

'What is Charite?' quod I þo. 'A childissh þinge', he seide;
    '*Nisi efficiamini sicut paruuli, non intrabitis in regnum celorum;*
Withouten fauntelte or foly, a fre liberal wille.'
    'Where shulde men fynde such a frende with so fre an herte? [445
I haue lyued in londe,' quod I; 'my name is Longe Wille,
And fonde I neuere ful charite bifore ne bihynde!
Men beth mercyable to mendynantz and to pore,
And wolen lene þere þei leue lelly to ben payed.
    Ac charite þat Poule preyseth best, and most plesaunte to owre
                                                    Saueoure, [450
    As, *non inflatur, non est ambiciosa, non querit que sua sunt,*
I seigh neuere such a man, so me God helpe,
That he ne wolde aske after his, and otherwhile coueyte
Þinge þat neded hym nouȝt, and nyme it if he myȝte!
Clerkis kenne me þat Cryst is in alle places;
Ac I seygh hym neuere sothly, but as myself in a miroure,   [455
    Ita in enigmate, tunc facie ad faciem.
And so I trowe trewly by þat men telleth of charite,
It is nought championes fyȝte, ne chaffare, as I trowe.'
    'Charite', quod he, 'ne chaffareth nouȝte, ne chalengeth, ne
                                                             craueth.

As proude of a peny as of a pounde of golde,
And is as gladde of a goune of a graye russet   [460
As of a tunicle of Tarse or of trye scarlet.
He is gladde with alle gladde and good tyl alle wykked,
And leueth and loueth alle þat owre Lorde made.
Curseth he no creature, ne he can bere no wratthe,
Ne no lykynge hath to lye, ne laughe men to scorne.   [465
Al þat men seith, he let it soth, and in solace taketh,
And alle manere meschiefs in myldenesse he suffreth;
Coueiteth he none erthly good, but heuene-riche blisse.'
    'Hath he any rentes or ricchesse, or any riche frendes?'
'Of rentes ne of ricchesse ne reccheth he neuere.   [470
For a frende þat fyndeth hym failled hym neuere at nede;

---

⁴⁵⁰ *inflatur:* MS *inflatus; est supplied*   ⁴⁶² tyl: MS ty

and forsake the flesh, I am wordless breath, and then I am called "Spirit". Both St Augustine and St Isidore gave me these names Now that you know them all, you can choose what you wish to call me.'

Then I asked: 'What is Charity?'

He replied: 'It is a freely generous disposition, childlike without being childish or foolish: "Unless you [turn and] become like children, you will never enter the kingdom of heaven".'

'Where is one to find such a generous-hearted friend?' I said. 'My name is Long Will. I have lived up and down the land, but I have never found perfect charity on any side. People are compassionate to beggars and to the poor, and are willing to lend when they expect scrupulous repayment, but the kind of charity which St Paul praises most highly and which most delights our Saviour, the charity which "is not arrogant or rude, does not insist on its own way"—God help me! I never met anyone like that, who would not demand what belonged to him and sometimes covet things of which he had no need and gain possession of them if he could. Scholars tell me that Christ is everywhere; but I have never truly seen Him—only as I see myself in a mirror: "For now we see in a mirror dimly, but then face to face". From what people say, I firmly believe that the same applies to charity. Certainly, to my mind, it is not present in champions' contests or in trading deals.'

'Charity', he said, 'drives no bargains, makes no claims, seeks for nothing. He is as proud of a penny as of a golden sovereign, and as pleased with a coarse grey woollen mantle as with a tunic of Tharsian silk or of rich scarlet. He rejoices with all who rejoice and is good to all the wicked, and trusts and loves all whom our Lord has made. He curses no one; he is incapable of bearing ill will; he has no taste for lying or for laughing men to scorn. He accepts whatever people say as true, and receives it with a light heart, and endures every kind of trouble uncomplainingly. He desires no earthly goods, but only the joy of the Kingdom of Heaven.'

'Has he any income? Any valuable possessions? Any wealthy friends?'

'He cares nothing for incomes or riches. He is supported by a friend who has never failed him in his need; "Thy will be

Fiat-voluntas-tua fynt hym euermore.
And if he soupeth, eet but a soppe of *spera-in-deo.*
He can purtreye wel þe *pater-noster* and peynte it with *aues,*
And otherwhile is his wone to wende in pilgrymage,   [475
Þere pore men and prisones liggeth, her pardoun to haue.
Þough he bere hem no bred, he bereth hem swetter lyflode,
Loueth hem as owre Lorde biddeth, and loketh how þei fare.
    And whan he is wery of þat werke, þanne wil he some tyme
Labory in a lauendrye wel þe lengthe of a myle,   [480
And ȝerne into ȝouthe and ȝepliche speke
Pryde with al þe appurtenaunce, and pakken hem togyderes,
And bouken hem at his brest and beten hem clene,
And leggen on longe with *laboraui-in-gemitu-meo,*
And with warme water at his eyghen wasshen hem after.   [485
And þanne he syngeth whan he doth so, and some tyme seith
                                                    wepyng,
    Cor contritum et humiliatum, deus, non despicies.'
    'By Cryst, I wolde þat I knewe hym,' quod I, 'no creature
                                                    leuere!'
'Withouten helpe of Piers Plowman', quod he, 'his persone seestow
                                                    neuere.'
'Where clerkes knowen hym', quod I, 'þat kepen holykirke?'
'Clerkes haue no knowyng', quod he, 'but by werkes and bi
                                                    wordes, [490
Ac Piers þe Plowman parceyueth more depper
What is þe wille and wherfore þat many wyȝte suffreth;
    Et vidit deus cogitaciones eorum.
For þere are ful proude-herted men paciente of tonge,
And boxome as of berynge to burgeys and to lordes,
And to pore peple han peper in þe nose,   [495
And as a lyoun he loketh þere men lakketh his werkes.
    For þere ar beggeres and bidderes, bedemen, as it were,
Loketh as lambren and semen lyf-holy,
Ac it is more to haue her mete with such an esy manere
Þan for penaunce and parfitnesse, þe pouerte þat such taketh. [500
Þerefore by coloure ne by clergye knowe shaltow hym neuere,
Noyther þorw wordes ne werkes, but þorw wille one.
And þat knoweth no clerke, ne creature in erthe,
But Piers þe Plowman, *Petrus, id est Christus.*
For he is nouȝte in lolleres, ne in lande-leperes hermytes, [505
Ne at ancres, þere a box hangeth; alle suche þei faiten.

---

⁴⁷³ eet: MS ette   ⁴⁹² What: MS þat   ⁴⁹⁷ bedemen: MS bedmen

done" keeps him perpetually supplied. When he dines, all he eats is a sop dipped in "Hope in God". He can write out the Lord's Prayer in a fair hand and decorate it with Hail Maries. He is accustomed to go on pilgrimage at other times to places where poor men are or where prisoners lie waiting to obtain their pardon. Although he brings them no bread, he brings them sweeter food; he loves them as our Lord commands and has a concern for their welfare.

'When he is tired of that work he will sometimes toil for a space in a laundry. He hastens to recollect his youth, addresses himself with vigour to pride and all the things that belong to it, and packs them together, lays them against his breast to steep and pounds them clean, labours on them for a long time with the words "I am weary with my moaning", then rinses them with hot tears. While he does this, he sings, and sometimes says, weeping: "A broken and contrite heart, O God, thou wilt not despise".'

'Christ! I desire to know him above all others', I said.

'Without the help of Piers the Ploughman,' he said, 'you will never behold him.'

'Can it be that the clergy, who have the care of Holy Church, do not know him?' I asked.

'The clergy's knowledge is based only on words and deeds,' he replied, 'but Piers the Ploughman can see more deeply into the heart's intentions and the reasons why many people show patience, like God, "knowing their thoughts". For there are men thoroughly proud at heart who speak patiently and behave meekly to burgesses and noblemen, but might have used pepper for snuff, they are so ready to take offence at poor people, and look as haughty as lions if their deeds are reproved. And there are beggars and those who solicit alms, seemingly men who pray for their benefactors, looking like lambs and apparently holy of life; but such men's poverty is assumed in order to get their food thus easily, rather than for penance or the desire for perfection. So you will never know Charity by his guise, nor by learning, nor by words or deeds, but only by the will of the heart—and that is known to no priest, nor to any living creature save Piers the Ploughman, "Peter, that is, Christ".

'Charity is not to be found in the company of vagabonds or roaming hermits, nor among anchorites with a begging box slung round them; all these are dissemblers. Cry shame on

Fy on faitoures and *in fautores suos*!
For Charyte is Goddis champioun, and as a good chylde hende,
And þe meryest of mouth at mete where he sitteth.
Þe loue þat lith in his herte maketh hym ly3te of speche,   [510]
And is companable and confortatyf as Cryst bit hymselue,
    Nolite fieri sicut ypocrite, tristes, etc.
For I haue seyn hym in sylke, and somme tyme in russet,
Bothe in grey and in grys and in gulte herneys,
And as gladlich he it gaf to gomes þat it neded.
Edmonde and Edwarde eyther were kynges,   [515]
And seyntes ysette tyl charite hem folwed.
I haue seyne Charite also syngen and reden,
Ryden and rennen in ragged wedes,
Ac biddyng as beggeres bihelde I hym neuere.
Ac in riche robes rathest he walketh,   [520]
Y-called and y-crimiled and his crowne shaue;
And in a freres frokke he was y-founde ones,
Ac it is ferre agoo, in seynt Fraunceys tyme;
In þat secte sitthe to selde hath he be knowen.
Riche men he recomendeth and of her robes taketh,   [525]
Þat withouten wyles leden her lyues,
    Beatus est diues, qui, etc.
In kynges courte he cometh ofte, þere þe conseille is trewe,
Ac if coueityse be of þe conseille, he wil nou3t come þerinne.
In courte amonge iaperes he cometh but selde,
For braulyng and bakbytyng and beryng of fals witnesse.   [530]
In þe constorie bifor þe comissarie he cometh nou3t ful ofte,
For her lawe dureth ouerlonge, but if þei lacchen syluer;
And matrimoigne for monye maken and vnmaken,
And þat conscience and Cryst hath y-knitte faste,
Þei vndon it vnworthily, þo doctours of lawe.   [535]
  Ac I ne lakke no lyf, but Lorde, amende vs alle,
And gyue vs grace, good God, charite to folwe!
For whoso my3te mete with hym, such maneres hym eyleth,
Noyther he blameth ne banneth, bosteth, ne prayseth,
Lakketh, ne loseth, ne loketh vp sterne,   [540]
Craueth, ne coueiteth, ne crieth after more;
    In pace in id-ipsum dormiam, etc.
Þe moste lyflode þat he lyueth by is loue in Goddis passioun;
Noyther he biddeth, ne beggeth, ne borweth to 3elde,
Misdoth he no man, ne with his mouth greueth.

---

[511] companable: MS compenable

such hypocrites and "on their patrons"! But Charity is God's knight, as courteous as a good-mannered child, and the merriest of speakers when he sits at table. The love that dwells in his heart makes him easy-spoken and good, cheerful company, in accordance with Christ's own bidding: "Do not look dismal, like hypocrites". I have seen him clad in silk and sometimes in rough cloth, in plain grey, in rich fur and in gilded armour; whichever he wore, he would give it with equal gladness to the needy. Both Edmund and Edward were kings, and were also reckoned as saints because Charity went in their train. I have also seen Charity chanting and reading the Bible, riding on horseback and going on foot in rags, but I never saw him in the guise of a beggar with his hand held out. But, most readily of all, he goes clad in rich vestments, wearing a skull cap and with his head anointed and tonsured. Once upon a time, he was to be found in a friar's habit, but that was long ago, in the days of St Francis. He has rarely been met with since in that Order. He commends rich men whose lives are free from guile, and accepts their garments, for "Blessed is the rich man who is found blameless and who does not go after gold". He often appears in the king's court when the council is honest, but he will not be present if covetousness is one of the councillors. He is seldom seen in the company of the court jesters, on account of their brawling and backbiting and lies. Neither does he often appear before the bishop's officer in the consistory court, for the doctors of law spin out their cases far too long, unless they are given a bribe, and make and unmake marriages in return for payment, dishonourably severing what Conscience and Christ have firmly knitted together.

'However, I blame nobody, but pray that the Lord God may amend us all and give us grace to follow Charity. For anyone who met him would find these characteristics in him: he does not blame others or call down curses on them, he is not boastful or laudatory, he neither censures nor flatters, he is not given to stern glances or to hankering or coveting or demanding more. He lives by the text "In peace I will both lie down and sleep [for thou alone, O Lord, makest me dwell in safety]". The chief food that sustains him is love, through the passion of God. He does not crave alms or beg or seek a loan, and he injures no one by deed or word.

Amonges Cristene men þis myldnesse shulde laste;   *[545*
In alle manere angres, haue þis at herte:
Þat, þough þei suffred al þis, God suffred for vs more,
In ensample we shulde do so, and take no veniaunce
Of owre foes þat doth vs falsenesse; þat is owre fadres wille.
For wel may euery man wite, if God hadde wolde hymselue,   *[550*
Sholde neuere Iudas ne Iuwe Iesu don on rode,
Ne han martired Peter ne Poule, ne in prisoun holden.
Ac he suffred in ensample þat we shulde suffre also,
And seide to suche þat suffre wolde þat *pacientes vincunt.*'

'Such gentleness should constantly exist among Christians. In every kind of affliction they should bear in mind that, whatever their sufferings, God suffered more for us, as an example to us to do likewise and to take no vengeance on our enemies who treat us falsely, for that is the will of our Father. For it is plain to all that, if God Himself had so desired, neither Judas nor any of the Jews might have set Jesus on the cross, nor martyred or imprisoned St Peter and St Paul. But He suffered to teach us that we, too, must suffer, and said to those who are willing to suffer that "the patient conquer".'

D

Wolleward and wete-shoed went I forth after,
As a reccheles renke þat of no wo reccheth,
And ȝede forth lyke a lorel al my lyf-tyme,
Tyl I wex wery of þe worlde and wylned eft to slepe,
And lened me to a lenten, and longe tyme I slepte,   [5
And of Crystes passioun and penaunce þe peple þat of-rauȝte,
Rested me þere, and rutte faste tyl *ramis-palmarum*;
Of gerlis and of *gloria laus* gretly me dremed,
And how osanna by orgonye olde folke songen.
One semblable to þe Samaritan and some-del to Piers þe Plowman
                                                                     [10

Barfote on an asse bakke botelees cam prykye,
Wythoute spores other spere, spakliche he loked,
As is þe kynde of a knyȝte þat cometh to be dubbed,
To geten hym gylte spores or galoches ycouped.
Þanne was Faith in a fenestre and cryde: 'A! *fili Dauid*!'   [15
As doth an heraude of armes whan auntrous cometh to iustes.
Olde Iuwes of Ierusalem for ioye þei songen
   Benedictus qui venit in nomine domini.
  Þanne I frayned at Faith what al þat fare be-mente,
And who sholde iouste in Iherusalem; 'Iesus,' he seyde,
'And fecche þat þe fende claymeth, Piers fruit þe Plowman.'   [20
'Is Piers in þis place?' quod I, and he preynte on me:
'Þis Iesus of his gentrice wole iuste in Piers armes,
In his helme and in his haberioun, *humana natura*;
Þat Cryst be nouȝt biknowe here for *consummatus deus*,
In Piers paltok þe Plowman þis priker shal ryde,   [25
For no dynte shal hym dere as *in deitate patris*.'
'Who shal iuste with Iesus?' quod I, 'Iuwes or scribes?'
'Nay,' quod he, 'þe foule fende and Fals-dome and Deth.
Deth seith he shal fordo and adown brynge
Al þat lyueth or loketh in londe or in watere.   [30
Lyf seyth þat he liketh and leyth his lif to wedde
Þat for al þat Deth can do, within þre dayes
To walke and fecche fro þe fende Piers fruite þe Plowman,
And legge it þere hym lyketh, and Lucifer bynde,
And forbete and adown brynge bale and deth for euere: [35
   O mors, ero mors tua!'

---

[11] prykye: MS pryke   [16] auntrous: MS aunturos   [18] be-mente: MS be ment
[24] consummatus: MS consumatus   [31] liketh: MS likthe   [35] and *supplied*

D: The Glory and the Aftermath

Then I went on my way, wet-shod and wearing harsh wool next to my skin after the fashion of a heedless man who cares nothing for discomfort. Day after day, I went about like a tramp until I grew weary of the world and yearned to sleep again. I drifted into Lent and slept for a long time, taking my rest in Christ's Passion and His penance, which reached out to cover all people, and snored soundly until Palm Sunday. I dreamed a great deal about children and their hymn 'All glory, laud and honour' and about how the old sang 'Hosanna', with chant and descant.

Someone who looked like the Good Samaritan, and somewhat like Piers the Ploughman, came riding barefoot, without boots, spurs, or spear, on the back of an ass. He had the eager look of one coming to be dubbed knight and to obtain golden spurs or slashed shoes. Faith stood at a window, crying out: 'Behold the Son of David!' like a herald-at-arms when knights come to tournaments. The old Jews of Jerusalem sang for joy: 'Blessed is he that cometh in the name of the Lord'.

Then I asked Faith what was the meaning of all this to-do, and who was to joust in Jerusalem.

'Jesus', he said, 'and He will bring away the fruit of Piers the Ploughman, which the devil lays claim to.'

'Is Piers here?' I asked. He gave me a glance.

'Jesus, as befits His noble lineage, will joust in Piers's armour, in his helmet and his coat of mail of Human Nature. This knight will ride in the doublet of Piers the Ploughman, so that Christ shall not be recognised here as Almighty God, for no stroke can harm Him in His Divine Nature.'

'Who is to joust with Jesus?' I asked. 'The Jews or the scribes?'

'No', he replied. 'The foul fiend and False Judgment and Death. Death says that he will destroy and overthrow every living thing on land or water. Life says that he is lying and stakes His life that, in spite of all that Death can do, He will arise and wrench Piers the Ploughman's fruit from the devil and place it where He chooses, and fetter Lucifer and beat down sorrow and death and overthrow them for ever: "O death, I will be thy death".'

H

Þanne cam *Pilatus* with moche peple, *sedens pro tribunali*,
To se how doughtilich Deth sholde do, and deme her botheres

riȝte.

Þe Iuwes and þe Iustice aȝeine Iesu þei were,
And al her courte on hym cryde *crucifige* sharpe.
Tho put hym forth a piloure bifor Pilat, and seyde: [40
'This Iesus of owre Iewes temple iaped and dispised,
To fordone it on o day, and in thre dayes after
Edefye it eft newe (here he stant þat seyde it),
And ȝit maken it as moche in al manere poyntes,
Bothe as longe and as large, bi loft and bi grounde.'   [45
'*Crucifige*,' quod a cacchepolle, 'I warante hym a wicche!'
'*Tolle, tolle!*' quod an other, and toke of kene thornes,
And bigan of kene thorne a gerelande to make,
And sette it sore on his hed, and seyde in envye:
'*Aue, Rabby!*' quod þat ribaude, and þrew redes at hym,   [50
Nailled hym with þre nailles naked on þe rode,
And poysoun on a pole þei put vp to his lippes,
And bede hym drynke his deth-yuel, his dayes were ydone.
'And ȝif þat þow sotil be, help now þiseluen;
If þow be Cryst, and kynges sone, come downe of þe rode;   [55
Þanne shul we leue þat Lyf þe loueth and wil nouȝt lete þe deye!'
'*Consummatum est*', quod Cryst, and comsed forto swowe
Pitousliche and pale as a prisoun þat deyeth;
Þe lorde of lyf and of liȝte þo leyed his eyen togideres.
Þe daye for drede withdrowe, and derke bicam þe sonne,   [60
Þe wal wagged and clef, and al þe worlde quaued.
Ded men for that dyne come out of depe graues,
And tolde whi þat tempest so longe tyme dured.
'For a bitter bataille', þe ded bodye sayde;
'Lyf and Deth in þis derknesse her one fordoth her other;   [65
Shal no wiȝte wite witterly who shal haue þe maystrye,
Er Sondey aboute sonne-rysynge'; and sank with þat til erthe.
Some seyde þat he was Goddes sone þat so faire deyde,
    Vere filius dei erat iste, etc.
And somme saide he was a wicche: 'Good is þat we assaye,
Where he be ded or nouȝte ded, doun er he be taken.'   [70
    Two theues also tholed deth þat tyme,
Vppon a crosse bisydes Cryst; so was þe comune lawe.
A cacchepole cam forth and craked bothe her legges,
And her armes after, of eyther of þo theues.

⁴⁷ of: MS O

Then came Pilate, accompanied by many people, and he 'was sitting on the judgment seat' to see what mighty deeds Death could perform and to adjudge the rights of both sides. The Jews and the judge opposed Jesus and all the court cried out in shrill tones for His crucifixion. Then a robber thrust himself forward before Pilate and said:

'This Jesus, who stands here, mocked our Jewish temple and poured scorn on it, saying that He would destroy it in one day and rebuild it anew three days later, making it just as great again in every way, as long and as broad above and below.'

'Crucify Him!' exclaimed a sergeant. 'I take my oath that He is a sorcerer.'

'Bear Him away, bear Him away!' cried another and, taking sharp thorns, he proceeded to make them into a crown, thrusting it painfully on to His head. 'Hail, Master!' he said with scoffing malice, and cast reeds at Him. They pinned Him naked to the cross with three nails, and thrust poison to His lips on a pole, bidding Him drink His death-draught, for His days were over. 'If you possess skilful arts, now help yourself! If you are Christ and a king's son, come down from the cross, and then we will believe that Life loves you and will not let you die!'

'It is finished', said Christ, and swooned, as pitiable and pale as a dying prisoner; and then the Lord of life and light closed His eyes. Daylight vanished for fear and the sun was darkened, the city wall rocked and splintered and the whole earth shook. Because of the tumult, dead men came out of their deep graves and revealed why the tempest was lasting so long.

'It is on account of a bitter fight', said one corpse. 'Life and Death are destroying each other here in this darkness. No one may know with certainty which one will be victorious until sunrise on Sunday.' With that, he sank back into the earth.

Some said that He who died so nobly was God's Son: 'Truly, this was the Son of God!' Others said that He was a necromancer, adding: 'It would be well for us to test whether He is dead or not before He is taken down.'

There were also two thieves who suffered death on the cross at the same time, at Christ's side, in accordance with the prevailing law. A legal officer strode forth and broke the legs, and then the arms, of each of these thieves, but no lout

Ac was no boy so bolde Goddes body to touche;   [75
For he was kny3te and kynges sone, kynde for3af þat tyme,
Þat non harlot were so hardy to leyne hande vppon hym.
Ac þere cam forth a kny3te, with a kene spere ygrounde,
Hi3te *Longeus*, as þe lettre telleth, and longe had lore his si3te.
Bifor Pilat and other peple in þe place he houed;   [80
Maugre his many tethe, he was made þat tyme
To take þe spere in his honde and iusten with Iesus;
For alle þei were vnhardy, þat houed on hors or stode,
To touche hym or to taste hym or take hym down of rode.
But þis blynde bacheler þanne bar hym þorugh þe herte;   [85
Þe blode spronge down by þe spere and vnspered þe kni3tes eyen.
Þanne fel þe kny3te vpon knees and cryed hym mercy:
'A3eyne my wille it was, Lorde, to wownde 3ow so sore!'
He seighed and sayde: 'Sore it me athynketh;
For þe dede þat I haue done, I do me in 3owre grace;   [90
Haue on me reuth, ri3tful Iesu!' and ri3t with þat he wept.
   Thanne gan Faith felly þe fals Iuwes dispise,
Called hem caytyues, acursed for euere
For þis foule vyleynye: 'Veniaunce to 3ow alle!
To do þe blynde bete hym ybounde, it was a boyes conseille.   [95
Cursed caytyue! kni3thod was it neuere
To mysdo a ded body, by day or by ny3te.
Þe gree 3it hath he geten, for al his grete wounde.
For 3owre champioun chiualer chief kny3t of 3ow alle
3elt hym recreaunt rennyng ri3t at Iesus wille.   [100
For be þis derkenesse ydo, his deth worth avenged,
And 3e, lordeynes, han ylost; for Lyf shal haue þe maistrye,
And 3owre fraunchise, þat fre was, fallen is in thraldome,
And 3e, cherles, and 3owre children chieue shal 3e neure,
Ne haue lordship in londe ne no londe tylye,   [105
But al bareyne be and vsurye vsen,
Which is lyf þat owre Lorde in alle lawes acurseth.
Now 3owre good dayes ar done, as Danyel prophecyed;
Whan Cryst cam, of her kyngdom the croune shulde cesse;
   Cum veniat sanctus sanctorum, cessabit vnxio vestra.'
   What for fere of þis ferly and of þe fals Iuwes,   [110
I drowe me in þat derkenesse to *decendit ad inferna.*
And þere I sawe sothely, *secundum scripturas,*
Out of þe west coste a wenche, as me thou3te,
Cam walkynge in þe wey; to-helle-ward she loked.

---

¹⁰⁹ of *supplied;* cesse *supplied*

had the hardihood to touch the body of God. Since He was a knight, and the son of a king, Nature granted on that occasion that no base man should presume to lay hands upon Him. However, as the story tells, a knight called Longinus, who had lost his sight long ago, appeared, carrying a sharply ground spear, and stood waiting there in front of Pilate and the rest of the people. In spite of his many protests, he was then forced to take his spear in his hand and to joust against Jesus; for all those who were present, on horseback or on foot, lacked the courage to handle or touch Him, or to take Him down from the cross. This blind knight, however, then ran Him through the heart. The blood gushed out and down along the spear and unsealed the knight's eyes, and he fell on his knees and besought His mercy.

'Lord,' he said, sighing, 'it was against my will that I wounded you so grievously. I bitterly repent what I have done and cast myself on your grace. Have pity on me, righteous Jesus!' And thereupon he wept.

Then Faith poured fierce contempt on the Jews for their perfidy, calling them miserable wretches, to be accursed in perpetuity for this foul wickedness. 'May vengeance light on all of you! It was a blackguard's trick to make a blind man strike Him, bound as He was. You damnable curs! The maltreatment of a dead body was never a part of knightly conduct. Yet, in spite of His great wound, He has gained the prize, for your champion rider, your principal knight, concedes his defeat in the lists and places himself at the disposal of Jesus. Once this darkness has passed, His death will be avenged and you, in your folly, have lost, for Life will have the upper hand and your former freedom is turned into slavery. Serfs! Neither you nor your children shall ever prosper, or be overlords, or cultivate the land, but live barrenly and exist by usury, which is a way of life condemned by our Lord in all His commandments. The days of your prosperity are over now, in accordance with Daniel's prophecy that, when Christ came, the crown of the kingdom would topple: "When the Holy of Holies shall come, your anointing shall cease".'

Through fear of the strange happenings and of the treacherous Jews I retreated, in the darkness, to where 'He descended into hell'. And there, 'according to the Scriptures', I saw a girl come walking along from the region of the west, with her gaze turned towards hell. This maiden was called

Mercy hiȝt þat mayde, a meke þynge withalle,   [115
A ful benygne buirde and boxome of speche.
Her suster, as it semed, cam softly walkynge,
Euene out of þe est, and westward she loked.
A ful comely creature, Treuth she hiȝte,
For þe vertue þat hir folwed, aferd was she neuere.   [120
Whan þis maydenes mette, Mercy and Treuth,
Eyther axed other of þis grete wonder,
Of þe dyne and of þe derknesse, and how þe daye rowed,
And which a liȝte and a leme lay befor helle.
'Ich haue ferly of þis fare, in feith,' seyde Treuth,   [125
'And am wendyng to wyte what þis wonder meneth.'
'Haue no merueille,' quod Mercy, 'myrthe it bytokneth.
A mayden þat hatte Marye, and moder without felyng
Of any kynnes creature, conceyued þorw speche
And grace of þe Holy Goste; wex grete with childe;   [130
Withouten wem into þis worlde she brouȝt hym;
And þat my tale be trewe, I take God to witnesse.
Sith þis barn was bore ben thritti wynter passed;
Which deyde and deth þoled þis day aboute mydday.
And þat is cause of þis clips þat closeth now þe sonne,   [135
In menynge þat man shal fro merkenesse be drawe,
Þe while þis liȝte and þis leme shal Lucyfer ablende.
For patriarkes and prophetes han preched herof often,
Þat man shal man saue þorw a maydenes helpe,
And þat was tynt þorw tre, tree shal it wynne,   [140
And þat deth doun brouȝte, deth shal releue.'
'Þat þow tellest', quod Treuth, 'is but a tale of Waltrot!
For Adam and Eue and Abraham, with other,
Patriarkes and prophetes, þat in peyne liggen,
Leue þow neuere þat ȝone liȝte hem alofte brynge,   [145
Ne haue hem out of helle; holde þi tonge, Mercy!
It is but a trufle þat þow tellest; I, Treuth, wote þe sothe.
For þat is ones in helle out cometh it neuere;
Iob þe prophete, patriarke, reproueth þi sawes,
      Quia in inferno nulla est redempcio.'
Þanne Mercy ful myldly mouthed þise wordes,   [150
'Thorw experience', quod she, 'I hope þei shal be saued.
For venym fordoth venym, and þat I proue by resoun.
For of alle venymes, foulest is þe scorpioun,
May no medcyne helpe þe place þere he styngeth,
Tyl he be ded and do þerto, þe yuel he destroyeth,   [155
Þe fyrst venymouste, þorw venym of hymself.

Mercy. She was an unassuming, sweet-natured lady, gentle in her speech. Her sister, as it appeared, came walking lightly from the east and looked westwards. She was a comely woman called Truth, totally without fear on account of the strength that attended her. When these maidens, Mercy and Truth, met, they questioned each other about this great marvel—the noise and the darkness, and how the day began to dawn, and what light and brightness hovered in front of hell.

Truth said: 'I am indeed bewildered by these happenings and I am on my way to discover what this strange sight may mean.'

'There is nothing to marvel at', said Mercy. 'It betokens joy. A virgin called Mary, a mother untouched by any mortal, conceived through the word and grace of the Holy Ghost. She became great with child and, immaculate, she brought Him into the world. God is my witness that my story is true. Thirty years have passed since the birth of this child who suffered death at noontide today. That is the cause of the eclipse which now envelops the sun, in token that mankind shall be drawn out of darkness and, at the same time, this light and brightness shall blind Lucifer. The patriarchs and the prophets have proclaimed many a time that Man shall save man by the help of a virgin, and that what was lost through a tree shall be won by a tree, and that what was brought down by death shall be raised up again by death.'

Truth said: 'All that you are saying is just an old wives' tale. Never think that that light can bear aloft Adam and Eve, Abraham and the rest, the patriarchs and prophets who lie in torment, or bring them out of hell. Hold your tongue, Mercy! Your words are mere frivolity; I, Truth, know what is true. Whatever is once in hell never comes out again. Job, the prophet and patriarch, disproves your words, saying: "So he who goes down to Sheol does not come up".'

Then Mercy replied with great gentleness, saying: 'Judging by experience, I trust that they *will* be saved, for, as I can prove by argument, poison destroys poison. The scorpion produces the most virulent of all poisons; no medicine can heal its sting until it is dead and placed against the spot, when, by its own poison, it destroys the evil effects of the original poison. So, I will stake my life, this particular death will undo

So shal þis deth fordo, I dar my lyf legge,
Al þat Deth fordyd furste þorw þe deuelles entysynge;
And riȝt as þorw gyle man was bigyled,
So shal grace þat bigan make a good sleighte;   [160
    Ars vt artem falleret.'
  'Now suffre we,' seyde Treuth, 'I se, as me þinketh,
Out of þe nippe of þe north, nouȝt ful fer hennes,
Riȝtwisnesse come rennynge; reste we þe while;
For he wote more þan we, he was er we bothe.'
'That is soth,' seyde Mercy, 'and I se here bi southe,   [165
Where Pees cometh playinge in pacience yclothed;
Loue hath coueyted hir longe; leue I none other
But he sent hir some lettre what þis liȝte bymeneth,
þat ouer-houeth helle þus; she vs shal telle.'
   Whan Pees, in pacience yclothed, approched nere hem tweyne,
                                   [170

Riȝtwisnesse her reuerenced for her riche clothyng,
And preyed Pees to telle hir to what place she wolde,
And in her gay garnementz whom she grete þouȝte?
'My wille is to wende', quod she, 'and welcome hem alle,
þat many day myȝte I nouȝte se for merkenesse of synne.   [175
Adam and Eue and other moo in helle,
Moyses and many mo mercy shal haue;
And I shal daunce þerto; do þow so, sustre!
For Iesus iusted wel, ioye bygynneth dawe;
    Ad vesperum demorabitur fletus, et ad matutinum leticia.
Loue, þat is my lemman, suche lettres me sente,   [180
That Mercy, my sustre, and I mankynde shulde saue;
And þat God hath forgyuen and graunted me, Pees, and Mercy,
To be mannes meynpernoure for eueremore after.
Lo! here þe patent!' quod Pees, '*in pace in idipsum—*
And þat þis dede shal dure—*dormiam et requiescam.'*   [185
  'What, rauestow?' quod Riȝtwisnesse, 'or þow art riȝt dronke!
Leuestow þat ȝonde liȝte vnlouke myȝte helle,
And saue mannes soule? sustre, wene it neure!
At þe bygynnynge, God gaf þe dome hymselue,
þat Adam and Eue and alle þat hem suwed   [190
Shulde deye doune riȝte and dwelle in pyne after,
If þat þei touched a tre and þe fruite eten.
Adam afterward, aȝeines his defence,
Frette of þat fruit and forsoke, as it were,

---

158 fordyd: MS dyd

all that was undone in the first place by Death, through the enticement of the devil; and just as mankind was tricked by trickery, so grace, which is the source of creation, will use cunning for good purposes, "art to deceive art".'

'Let us pause a while', said Truth. 'It seems to me that, not very far away, I see Righteousness hurrying out of the piercing cold of the north. Let us wait until she comes, for she is wiser than we are; she existed before both of us.'

'That is true,' said Mercy, 'and, to the south, I see Peace, dressed in patience, coming on dancing feet. Love has desired her for a long time; I have no doubt at all that he has written to tell her the meaning of this light that hovers over hell. She will inform us.'

When Peace, dressed in patience, drew nearer to the two of them, Righteousness greeted her respectfully, on account of the splendour of her garments, and besought Peace to tell her where she was going in her bright raiment, and whom she intended to greet.

She said: 'My intention is to go and welcome all those whom I have been unable to see for many a day because of the darkness of sin. Adam and Eve, Moses and many others also who are in hell shall obtain mercy, and at that I shall dance; my sister, do likewise! Joy is beginning to dawn because Jesus fought well in the lists: "Weeping may tarry for the night, but joy comes with the morning". Love, my sweetheart, has sent me letters to say that my sister Mercy and I are to save mankind and that God has fully granted and allowed that I, Peace, and Mercy shall be mankind's surety for ever after. Look, here is the authorisation!' said Peace. 'And the assurance that the deed is lasting: "In peace I will both lie down and sleep".'

'Are you mad or drunk?' said Righteousness. 'Do you believe that that light can unlock hell and save man's soul? Think no such thing, my sister! In the beginning, God Himself decreed that Adam and Eve and all their descendants should utterly perish and subsequently dwell in torment, if they laid hands on a certain tree and ate its fruit. Disregarding His prohibition, Adam later devoured that fruit and forsook

þe loue of owre Lorde and his lore bothe,   [195
And folwed þat þe fende tauȝte and his felawes wille,
Aȝeines resoun; I, Riȝtwisnesse, recorde þus with treuth,
Þat her peyne be perpetuel and no preyere hem helpe.
Forþi late hem chewe as þei chose and chyde we nouȝt, sustres,
For it is botelees bale, þe bite þat þei eten.'   [200
    'And I shal preue', quod Pees, 'her peyne mote haue ende,
And wo into wel mowe wende atte laste;
For had þei wist of no wo, wel had þei nouȝte knowen.
For no wiȝte wote what wel is þat neuere wo suffred,
Ne what is hote hunger, þat had neuere defaute.   [205
If no nyȝte ne were, no man, as I leue,
Shulde wite witterly what day is to mene;
Shulde neuere riȝte riche man þat lyueth in reste and ese
Wyte what wo is, ne were þe deth of kynde.
So God, þat bygan al, of his good wille   [210
Bycam man of a mayde mankynde to saue,
And suffred to be solde, to see þe sorwe of deyinge,
The which vnknitteth al kare and comsynge is of reste.
For til *modicum* mete with vs, I may it wel avowe,
Wote no wiȝte, as I wene, what is ynough to mene.   [215
    Forþi God of his goodnesse þe fyrste gome, Adam,
Sette hym in solace and in souereigne myrthe;
And sith he suffred hym synne, sorwe to fele,
To wite what wel was kyndelich to knowe it.
And after God auntred hymself, and toke Adames kynde,   [220
To wyte what he hath suffred in þre sondri places,
Bothe in heuene, and in erthe, and now til helle he þynketh,
To wite what al wo is, þat wote of al ioye.
So it shal fare bi þis folke; her foly and her synne
Shal lere hem what langour is, and lisse withouten ende.   [225
Wote no wighte what werre is, þere þat pees regneth,
Ne what is witterly wel, til weyllowey hym teche.'
    Thanne was þere a wiȝte with two brode eyen,
Boke hiȝte þat beupere, a bolde man of speche.
'By Godes body,' quod this Boke, 'I wil bere witnesse,   [230
Þat þo þis barne was ybore þere blased a sterre,
That alle þe wyse of þis worlde in o witte acordeden,
That such a barne was borne in Bethleem citee,
Þat mannes soule sholde saue, and synne destroye.
And alle þe elementz', quod þe Boke, 'herof bereth witnesse.   [235

---

201 I *supplied*

both our Lord's love and His teaching and, contrary to reason, followed the devil's doctrine and his wife's desire. I, Righteousness, bear true witness that their torment will be without end and that no prayer will help them. So, my sisters, let them chew their chosen food and let us not quarrel, for what they bit and swallowed is sorrow past remedy.'

'And I', said Peace, 'will prove that their suffering may have an end, sorrow at last be turned into joy. If they had never experienced sorrow, they could not have known joy, for a man who has never endured sorrow cannot know the nature of joy, nor can one who has never lacked food know what keen hunger is. If there were no night, no one would have any certain knowledge of what daylight means. A wealthy man, who lives amid leisure and comfort, would never know what sorrow is, if it were not for death, that comes by nature. So God, who created all things, in the goodness of His will became incarnate through a virgin in order to save mankind, and allowed Himself to be delivered up to experience the sorrow of death, which unravels all anxiety and is the beginning of rest. For until scant rations come our way, no one, I think, knows the meaning of sufficiency.

'So, in His goodness, God placed the first man, Adam, amid comfort and supreme happiness, and later permitted him to sin in order to experience sorrow and come to intimate knowledge of it, so that he might learn what happiness is. Afterwards, God took up the challenge Himself and assumed Adam's nature, to learn what he has suffered in three separate places: in heaven, on earth and now, as His intention is, in hell, so that He who knows the fullness of joy may know the fullness of sorrow. So it will happen to this people; their folly and sin will teach them what suffering is and what endless happiness is. No one can grasp what war is like when peace holds sway, or what true well-being is like until the cry of despair brings him realisation.'

Then there appeared a man with two wide-open eyes, a reverend man called Book, fearless in his speech.

This Book said: 'By God! I will bear witness that, when this child was born, a star blazed out, so that all the wise men in the world agreed, with one accord, that a child was born in the city of Bethlehem of such nature that He would save man's soul and destroy sin. All the elements', Book continued, 'bear witness to this. First of all, the sky revealed that He was

þat he was God þat al wrou3te, þe walkene firste shewed;
Þo that weren in heuene token *stella comata*,
And tendeden hir as a torche to reuerence his birthe;
Þe ly3te folwed þe Lorde into þe lowe erthe.
Þe water witnessed þat he was God, for he went on it;   [240
Peter þe apostel parceyued his gate,
And as he went on þe water wel hym knewe, and seyde,
    Iube me venire ad te super aquas.
And lo! how þe sonne gan louke her li3te in herself,
Whan she seye hym suffre þat sonne and se made!
The erthe, for heuynesse that he wolde suffre,   [245
Quaked as quykke þinge, and al biquashte the roche!
Lo! helle mi3te nou3te holde, but opened þo God þoled,
And lete oute Symondes sones to seen hym hange on rode.
And now shal Lucifer leue it, thowgh hym loth þinke:
For *Gygas* þe geaunt, with a gynne engyned   [250
To breke and to bete doune þat ben a3eines Iesus.
And I, Boke, wil be brent but Iesus rise to lyue,
In alle my3tes of man and his moder gladye,
And conforte al his kynne and out of care brynge,
And al þe Iuwen ioye vnioignen and vnlouken;   [255
And, but þei reuerencen his rode and his resurexioun,
And bileue on a new lawe, be lost lyf and soule.'
   'Suffre we,' seide Treuth, 'I here and se bothe,
How a spirit speketh to helle and bit vnspere þe 3atis;
    Attollite portas, etc.'
A voice loude in þat li3te to Lucifer cryeth,   [260
'Prynces of þis place, vnpynneth and vnlouketh!
For here cometh with croune þat kynge is of glorie.'
Thanne syked Sathan and seyde to hem alle,
'Suche a ly3te a3eines owre leue Lazar it fette;
Care and combraunce is comen to vs alle.   [265
If þis kynge come in, mankynde wil he fecche,
And lede it þer hym lyketh and ly3tlych me bynde.
Patriarkes and prophetes han parled herof longe,
Þat such a lorde and a ly3te shulde lede hem alle hennes.'
   'Lysteneth,' quod Lucifer, 'for I þis Lorde knowe,   [270
Bothe þis Lorde and þis li3te; is longe ago I knewe hym.
May no deth hym dere, ne no deueles queyntise,
And where he wil, is his waye; ac war hym of þe periles;
If he reue me my ri3te, he robbeth me by maistrye.

---

240 þe: MS þat   **246** biquashte: MS biquasht

God, the creator of all things. The celestial beings took a
comet and kindled it like a torch to pay homage to His birth,
and the light followed the Lord down to the earth beneath.
The water testified that He was God, because He walked upon
it. The Apostle Peter saw what path He took and recognised
Him as He trod on the water, and said: "Bid me come to you
on the water". And behold how the sun withdrew its light
into itself when it saw the Passion of the Maker of sun and sea!
The earth, through grief at His suffering, trembled like a live
creature, and the rocks shattered to pieces. Hell could not hold
firm, but opened when God suffered and released the sons of
Simeon to see Him hanging on the cross. And now Lucifer
will have to believe this, however much against his will, for
Jesus the giant has contrived a battering-ram with which to
shatter and beat down those who oppose Him. I, Book, will
go to the stake if Jesus does not rise to life with all His bodily
powers, bringing joy to His mother, and comfort and release
from sorrow to His kindred, and destroying and undoing all
the happiness of the Jews. Unless they pay homage to His
cross and His resurrection and believe in a new law, they will
perish in body and soul.'

'Wait!' said Truth. 'I hear and see a spirit who addresses
hell and orders the gates to be unbarred, saying: "Lift up
your heads, O gates! [and be lifted up, O ancient doors!
that the King of glory may come in!]".'

From the heart of that light a voice called to Lucifer, saying:
'You rulers of this place, undo your bolts and locks, for the
crowned King of glory approaches.'

Then Satan, sighing, said to them all: 'Against our will, a
light like this carried away Lazarus. Sorrow and trouble are
come upon us all. If this king enters, He will bear mankind
away and lead them where it pleases Him, and bind me with
ease. Patriarchs and prophets have talked about this for a long
time, saying that a lord and a light like this would lead them
all hence.'

'Listen to me!' said Lucifer. 'I know this lord, and this
light, too, of old. Death cannot harm Him, nor any devil's
cunning. His path lies where He chooses; but let Him beware
of the perils! If He deprives me of my rights, He robs me by
the force of power, for according to what is right and reason-

For by ri3t and bi resoun, þo renkes þat ben here,   [275
Bodye and soule, ben myne, bothe gode and ille.
For hymself seyde, þat sire is of heuene,
3if Adam ete þe apple, alle shulde deye,
And dwelle with vs deueles; þis þretynge he made;
And he þat sothenesse is seyde þise wordes;   [280
And sitthen I seised seuene hundreth wyntre,
I leue þat lawe nil nau3te lete hym þe leest.'
'That is sothe,' seyde Sathan, 'but I me sore drede,
For þow gete hem with gyle and his gardyne breke,
And in semblaunce of a serpent sat on þe appeltre,   [285
And eggedest hem to ete, Eue by hirselue,
And toldest hir a tale, of tresoun were þe wordes;
And so þow haddest hem oute and hider atte laste.
It is nou3te graythely geten, þere gyle is the rote.'
'For God wil nou3t be bigiled', quod Gobelyn, 'ne bi-iaped;   [290
We haue no trewe title to hem, for þorwgh tresoun were þei
                                              dampned.'
'Certes, I drede me', quod þe deuel, 'leste treuth wil hem fecche.
Þis þretty wynter, as I wene, hath he gone and preched;
I haue assailled hym with synne, and some tyme y-asked
Where he were God or Goddes sone? He gaf me shorte answere.
                                              [295
And þus hath he trolled forth þis two and thretty wynter,
And whan I seighe it was so, slepyng, I went
To warne Pilates wyf what dones man was Iesus;
For Iuwes hateden hym and han done hym to deth.
I wolde haue lengthed his lyf, for I leued, 3if he deyede,   [300
That his soule wolde suffre no synne in his sy3te.
For þe body, whil it on bones 3ede, aboute was euere
To saue men fram synne, 3if hemself wolde.
And now I se where a soule cometh hiderward seyllynge
With glorie and with grete li3te; God it is, I wote wel.   [305
I rede we flee', quod he, 'faste alle hennes,
For vs were better nou3te be þan biden his sy3te.
For þi lesynges, Lucifer, loste is al owre praye.
Firste þorw þe we fellen fro heuene so heighe;
For we leued þi lesynges, we loupen oute alle with þe,   [310
And now, for thi last lesynge, ylore we haue Adam,
And al owre lordeship, I leue, a londe and a water;
          Nunc princeps huius mundi eicietur foras.'

---

310 f. we loupen . . . last lesynge *supplied*

able, the people here, good and bad alike, are mine, body and soul. For the Lord of Heaven Himself pronounced the threat that, if Adam ate the apple, all should die and dwell among us devils, and He who said this is Truth. Since I have been in possession for seven hundred years, I do not believe that lawful judgment will accord Him the least of them.'

'That is true,' said Satan, 'but I am greatly afraid, because you acquired them by guile. You broke into His garden, and coiled up on the apple-tree in the form of a serpent. You incited them to eat, approaching Eve on her own and telling her a tale couched in treacherous words. By these means you got them out, and, at last, away here. When guile is at the root of it, there is no fair acquisition.'

'God will not be deceived or mocked', said Hobgoblin. 'We have no true title to them, because they were damned through treachery.'

'I am indeed afraid', said the devil, 'that Truth will carry them off. He has gone about preaching for the last thirty years. I have tempted Him to sin and asked Him once whether He was God, or the Son of God? He gave me a short answer. He has continued in this way for the last thirty-two years. When I saw how it was, I went and warned Pilate's wife in her sleep what manner of man Jesus was, for the Jews hated Him and have put Him to death. I wanted to lengthen His life because I believed that, if He died, His soul would not permit sin to exist in His presence, since His fleshly body was constantly occupied in saving men from sin, if they were willing. Now I behold a soul coming quickly towards us in glory and great light. I know that this is God. My advice', he said, 'is that we should all flee quickly away, for it would be better for us not to exist than to let Him see us. All our prey is lost, Lucifer, on account of your lies. It was through you that we fell in the first place from the heavenly heights; we all hurtled down with you because we believed your lies. Now, because of your latest lie, I believe we have lost Adam and all our sovereignty on land and sea: "Now shall the ruler of this world be cast out".'

Efte þe liȝte bad vnlouke, and Lucifer answered:
'What lorde artow?' quod Lucifer, '*quis est iste?*'
'*Rex glorie*', þe liȝte sone seide,   [315
'And lorde of myȝte and of mayne and al manere vertues,
    dominus virtutum.
Dukes of þis dym place, anon vndo þis ȝates,
That Cryst may come in, þe kynges sone of heuene.'
And with þat breth helle brake, with Beliales barres;
For any wye or warde wide opene þe ȝatis.   [320
Patriarkes and prophetes, *populus in tenebris*,
Songen seynt Iohanes songe, '*ecce agnus dei*'.
Lucyfer loke ne myȝte, so lyȝte hym ableynte;
And þo þat owre Lorde loued into his liȝte he lauȝte,
And seyde to Sathan: 'Lo! here my soule to amendes   [325
For alle synneful soules, to saue þo þat ben worthy.
Myne þei be, and of me; I may þe bette hem clayme.
Alþough resoun recorde, and riȝt of myself,
That if þei ete the apple, alle shulde deye,
I bihyȝte hem nouȝt here helle for euere.   [330
For þe dede þat þei dede, þi deceyte it made;
With gyle þow hem gete agayne al resoun.
For in my paleys, paradys, in persone of an addre
Falseliche þow fettest þere þynge þat I loued.
Thus ylyke a lusarde with a lady visage,   [335
Theuelich þow me robbedest; þe olde lawe graunteth
Þat gylours be bigiled, and þat is gode resoun;
    Dentem pro dente, et oculum pro oculo.
Ergo, soule shal soule quyte and synne to synne wende,
And al þat man hath mysdo I, man, wyl amende.
Membre for membre bi þe olde lawe was amendes,   [340
And lyf for lyf also, and by þat lawe I clayme it,
Adam and al his issue at my wille herafter.
And þat deth in hem fordid my deth shal releue,
And bothe quykke and quyte þat queynte was þorw synne;
And þat grace gyle destruye, good feith it asketh.   [345
So leue it nouȝte, Lucifer, aȝeine þe lawe I fecche hem,
But bi riȝt and by resoun raunceoun here my lyges:
    Non veni soluere legem, sed adimplere.
Þow fettest myne in my place aȝeines al resoun,
Falseliche and felounelich; gode faith me it tauȝte,
To recoure hem thorw raunceoun and bi no resoun elles.   [350

324 Lorde *supplied*

Then the light commanded that the locks be undone, and Lucifer answered, saying: 'What manner of lord are you? "Who is this?".'

The light said, straightway: ' "The king of glory", the lord of power and might and strength of every kind, "the Lord, strong and mighty". You rulers of this place of shadows, unbar these gates at once, so that Christ, the Son of the King of heaven, may come in!'

At the sound of that voice, hell and the bars set up by Belial snapped, and the gates burst wide open, in spite of all the watchmen and keepers. The patriarchs and the prophets, 'the people who sat in darkness', sang the song of St John the Baptist: 'Behold the Lamb of God!' Lucifer was so blinded by light that he could not see, and our Lord snatched up those whom He loved into His light, saying to Satan:

'Here is my soul as the ransom price for all sinful souls, that those who are worthy may be saved. They are mine, and came from me; I have the better claim to them. Although reason and my own justice may lay it down that, if they ate the apple, all should die, I did not consign them to hell for ever, for what they did was brought about by your deceit. You gained possession of them by guile, against all the laws of reason. In the form of an adder, you carried off, by false means, that which I loved from paradise, my palace. In the guise of a serpent with a woman's face you robbed me like a thief. The old law permits deceivers to be deceived, and that is sound reasoning. "An eye for an eye and a tooth for a tooth". Therefore, soul shall pay quittance for soul, and sin shall parry sin, and I, as man, will make amends for all that man has done amiss. According to the old law, limb for limb and life for life constituted satisfaction, and on that law I base my claim to Adam and all his issue at my desire from now on. My death shall restore what death destroyed in them and rekindle and redeem that which was quenched by sin. Honesty requires that grace should destroy guile, so do not think, Lucifer, that I am bearing them away unlawfully; I am now ransoming my subjects in accordance with justice and reason, for "I have not come to abolish the law, but to fulfil it". Contrary to all reason, you carried off my people in my territory by a false felon's act; honesty prompted me to win them back by simple ransom, so that what you acquired by guile is retrieved by grace. You, Lucifer, in the guise of an

I

So þat with gyle þow gete, þorw grace it is ywone.
Þow, Lucyfer, in lyknesse of a luther addere,
Getest by gyle þo that God loued;
And I, in lyknesse of a leode, þat Lorde am of heuene,
Graciousliche þi gyle haue quytte; go gyle aʒeine gyle!   [355
And as Adam and alle þorw a tre deyden,
Adam and alle þorwe a tree shal torne aʒeine to lyue;
And gyle is bigyled and in his gyle fallen:
    Et cecidit in foueam quam fecit.
Now bygynneth þi gyle ageyne þe to tourne,
And my grace to growe ay gretter and wyder.   [360
Þe bitternesse þat þow hast browe, brouke it þiseluen,
Þat art doctour of deth, drynke þat þow madest!
   For I, þat am Lorde of lyf, loue is my drynke,
And for þat drynke to-day I deyde vpon erthe.
I fauʒte so, me þrestes ʒet for mannes soule sake;   [365
May no drynke me moiste ne my thruste slake,
Tyl þe vendage falle in þe vale of Iosephath,
Þat I drynke riʒte ripe must, *resureccio mortuorum*,
And þanne shal I come as a kynge crouned with angeles,
And han out of helle alle mennes soules.   [370
   Fendes and fendekynes bifor me shulle stande,
And be at my biddynge whereso eure me lyketh.
And to be merciable to man þanne my kynde it asketh;
For we beth bretheren of blode, but nouʒte in baptesme alle.
Ac alle þat beth myne hole bretheren, in blode and in baptesme,
                                                               [375
Shal nouʒte be dampned to þe deth þat is withouten ende;
    Tibi soli peccaui, etc.
It is nouʒt vsed in erthe to hangen a feloun
Ofter þan ones, þough he were a tretour.
And ʒif þe kynge of þat kyngedome come in þat tyme,
There þe feloun thole sholde deth or otherwyse,   [380
Lawe wolde, he ʒeue hym lyf if he loked on hym.
And I, þat am kynge of kynges, shal come suche a tyme,
There dome to þe deth dampneth al wikked;
And ʒif lawe wil I loke on hem, it lithe in my grace,
Whether þei deye or deye nouʒte for þat þei deden ille.   [385
Be it any þinge abouʒte þe boldenesse of her synnes,
I may do mercy þorw riʒtwisnesse, and alle my wordes trewe.
And þough holiwrit wil þat I be wroke of hem þat deden ille,
    Nullum malum inpunitum, etc.,
Thei shul be clensed clereliche and wasshen of her synnes

evil adder guilefully gained possession of those whom God loved: I, the Lord of Heaven, in man's guise have settled the score of your guile by means of grace. Let guile counter guile! Just as Adam and all mankind died because of a tree, so Adam and all mankind shall be restored to life because of a tree. Deceit is deceived and fallen into its own deceiving: "He [makes a pit, digging it out, and] falls into the hole which he has made".

'Now your wiles begin to turn against you, and my grace begins to spread ever more greatly and widely. You have brewed a bitter cup; quaff it yourself! You are death's physician; drink your own potion! As for me, who am the Lord of life, my drink is love, and, on account of that drink, I died on earth today. I fought so hard for the sake of man's soul that I am still thirsty. No liquor can moisten my parched throat or quench my thirst until the vintage matures in the valley of Jehoshaphat, to let me drink deep of the ripe new wine of "the resurrection of the dead". Then I will come as a king, angel-crowned, and bring the souls of all men out of hell. Devils great and small shall stand before me and go wherever I please, at my command. My nature demands that I should be merciful to mankind at that time, for we are blood-brothers, though not all brothers in baptism. But all those who are my full brothers, by blood and by baptism, shall not be condemned to everlasting death. As the Psalm says: "Against thee, thee only, have I sinned [and done that which is evil in thy sight]".

'It is not the custom on earth to hang a felon more than once, not even if he is a traitor; and if the king of the realm comes by at the time when the felon is due to die, or to suffer some other punishment, the law holds that, if he turns his glance on the man, he may grant him his life. So I, who am King of kings, will come by at a time like that, when judgment condemns all evildoers to death. If it is lawful for me to turn my glance upon them, then it is at the disposal of my grace to decide whether they should or should not die for their misdeeds.

'If the presumption of their sins is in the smallest measure paid for, I can, in rightful justice, show mercy without impairing the truth of my words. Even though Holy Scripture demands that I should take vengeance on those who have done evil, saying: "No evil shall go unpunished", they shall be washed bright and cleansed from their sins in my prison,

In my prisoun, purgatorie, til *parce* it hote,   [390
And my mercy shal be shewed to manye of my bretheren.
For blode may suffre blode bothe hungry and akale,
Ac blode may nouȝt se blode blede, but hym rewe.'—
    Audiui archana verba, que non licet homini loqui.—
Ac my riȝtwisnesse and riȝt shal reulen al helle,
And mercy al mankynde bifor me in heuene.   [395
For I were an vnkynde kynge, but I my kynde holpe,
And namelich at such a nede þer nedes helpe bihoueth;
    Non intres in iudicium cum seruo tuo, domine.
Þus bi lawe', quod owre Lorde, 'lede I wil fro hennes
Þo þat me loued, and leued in my comynge.
And for þi lesynge, Lucifer, þat þow lowe til Eue,   [400
Thow shalt abye it bittre'—and bonde hym with cheynes.
Astaroth and al þe route hidden hem in hernes,
They dorste nouȝte loke on owre Lorde, þe boldest of hem alle,
But leten hym lede forth what hym lyked and lete what hym liste.
    Many hundreth of angeles harpeden and songen,   [405
     Culpat caro, purgat caro; regnat deus dei caro.
Thanne piped pees of poysye a note,
'*Clarior est solito post maxima nebula phebus,*
Post inimicitias clarior est et amor.
After sharpe shoures', quod Pees, 'moste shene is þe sonne;
Is no weder warmer þan after watery cloudes,   [410
Ne no loue leuere ne leuer frendes
Þan after werre and wo, whan Loue and Pees be maistres.
Was neuere werre in þis worlde, ne wykkednesse so kene,
Þat ne Loue, and hym luste, to laughynge ne brouȝte,
And Pees þorw pacience alle perilles stopped.'   [415
'Trewes,' quod Treuth, 'þow tellest vs soth, bi Iesus!
Clippe we in couenaunt and vch of vs cusse other!'
'And lete no peple', quod Pees, 'perceyue þat we chydde!
For inpossible is no þyng to hym þat is almyȝty.'
'Thow seist soth', seyde Ryȝtwisnesse, and reuerentlich hir kyste,
                                                [420

Pees, and Pees here, *per secula seculorum.*
    Misericordia et veritas obuiauerunt sibi; iusticia et pax osculate sunt.
Treuth tromped þo, and songe '*Te deum laudamus*';
And thanne luted Loue in a loude note,
    Ecce quam bonum et quam iocundum, etc.
  Tyl þe daye dawed, þis damaiseles daunced,

---

408 *clarior est et amor supplied:* MS *etc.*

Purgatory, until compassion cries halt. My mercy will be shown to many of my brothers, for though one bound by the blood-tie can endure the sight of those of the same blood suffering hunger and cold, he cannot, with equanimity, watch those of the same blood bleed; I have heard "things that cannot be told, which man may not utter". My justice and righteousness shall hold sway throughout hell, and my mercy shall hold sway over all mankind ranged before me in heaven, for I should be an unnatural king if I did not help my natural kindred, and particularly at such a time of need, when, needs must, help should be given: "Enter not into judgment with thy servant". So,' our Lord said, 'in accordance with law I will lead away from here those who love me and had faith in my coming, and you, Lucifer, shall pay a bitter penalty for the falseness of your lie to Eve'—and He bound him in fetters.

Astaroth and the rest of the rabble concealed themselves in hiding places. Not even the boldest of them dared to set eyes on our Lord, but allowed Him to lead forth those whom He chose to and leave behind those whom He wished. Many hundreds of angels harped and sang: 'Flesh sins, flesh expiates, flesh reigns as God of God'. Then Peace fluted a song: 'The sun is always brighter after the thickest clouds, and love is brighter after enmity.'

'The sun shines brightest after sharp showers,' said Peace, 'and there is no warmer weather than that which follows drizzling clouds, and no dearer love or closer friendship than when Love and Peace rule, after strife and sorrow. There was never yet any strife or evil so sharp that Love could not, at his pleasure, transform it into laughter, and Peace, by patience, bring all dangers to an end.'

'Call a truce!' said Truth. 'Before God, what you tell us is true! Let us embrace and kiss each other in token of agreement.'

'And let no one see that we disagreed,' said Peace, 'for nothing is impossible to the Almighty.'

'You speak truly', said Righteousness, and kissed Peace reverently, and Peace kissed her, 'forever and ever'. 'Mercy and truth are met together: righteousness and peace have kissed each other.'

Then Truth sounded a trumpet and sang 'We praise thee, O God!' and Love played in loud tones on her lute: 'Behold, how good and pleasant it is [when brothers dwell in unity]!'.

These maidens danced until the dawn of day, when the

That men rongen to þe resurexioun; and riȝt with þat I waked,

[425

And called Kitte my wyf, and Kalote my douȝter—
'Ariseth and reuerenceth Goddes resurrexioun,
And crepeth to þe crosse on knees and kisseth it for a iuwel,
For Goddes blissed body it bar for owre bote.
And it afereth þe fende, for suche is þe myȝte   [430
May no grysly gost glyde þere it shadweth!'

   Thus I awaked and wrote what I had dremed,
And diȝte me derely and dede me to cherche,
To here holy þe masse and to be houseled after.
In myddes of þe masse, þo men ȝede to offrynge,   [435
I fel eftsones aslepe, and sodeynly me mette
That Pieres þe Plowman was paynted al blody
And come in with a crosse bifor þe comune peple,
And riȝte lyke in alle lymes to owre Lorde Iesu;
And þanne called I Conscience to kenne me þe sothe.   [440
'Is þis Iesus þe iuster?' quod I, 'þat Iuwes did to deth?
Or it is Pieres þe Plowman? Who paynted hym so rede?'
Quod Conscience, and kneled þo: 'þise aren Pieres armes,
His coloures and his cote-armure, ac he þat cometh so blody
Is Cryst with his crosse, conqueroure of Crystene.'   [445
   'Why calle ȝe hym Cryst?' quod I, 'sithenes Iuwes calle hym
                                              Iesus?

Patriarkes and prophetes prophecyed bifore
Þat alkyn creatures shulden knelen and bowen
Anon as men nempned þe name of God, Iesu.
Ergo is no name to þe name of Iesus,   [450
Ne none so nedeful to nempne by nyȝte ne by daye.
For alle derke deuelles aren adradde to heren it,
And synful aren solaced and saued by þat name.
And ȝe callen hym Cryst; for what cause, telleth me?
Is Cryst more of myȝte and more worthy name   [455
Þan Iesu or Iesus, þat al owre ioye come of?'
   'Thow knowest wel', quod Conscience, 'and þow konne resoun,
That knyȝte, kynge, conqueroure may be o persone.
To be called a kniȝte is faire, for men shal knele to hym;
To be called a kynge is fairer, for he may knyȝtes make;   [460
Ac to be conquerour called, þat cometh of special grace,
And of hardynesse of herte and of hendenesse bothe,

---

bells pealed for the Resurrection—and at that I awoke, and
called to my wife, Kit, and my daughter, Kalot: 'Arise, and
pay homage to God's resurrection and approach the cross on
your knees and kiss it as a precious jewel, because it bore the
blessed body of God for our redemption. It puts the devil to
fright, for its power is so great that no wicked spirit may come
beneath its shade.'

So I awoke and wrote down what I had dreamed, then
dressed myself in my best and went to church to hear the
whole of Mass and afterwards make my Communion. Half-
way through Mass, when the congregation went up with the
offertory, I fell asleep again, and suddenly dreamed that Piers
the Ploughman, all daubed with blood, came in carrying a
cross in front of the people, looking in every respect exactly
like our Lord Jesus. Then I called on Conscience for true
enlightenment.

'Is this Jesus the champion, whom the Jews put to death?'
I asked, 'or is it Piers the Ploughman? Who dyed him so
red?'

Kneeling, Conscience replied: 'These are Piers's arms and
colours and coat-armour, but He who comes thus covered
with blood is Christ with His cross, conqueror of Christen-
dom.'

'Why do you call Him Christ,' I said, 'seeing that the Jews
call Him Jesus? The patriarchs and prophets earlier foretold
that all creation should straightway kneel and bow down at
the naming of the Name of God—"Jesus". Therefore no name
can compare with the name of Jesus, and there is no name so
necessary to pronounce, night and day, for all the devils of
darkness dread the sound of it, and by that name sinners are
comforted and saved. Yet you call Him "Christ". Tell me
why! Is "Christ" a more powerful or more honourable name
than that of "Jesus", from which all our joy is derived?'

Conscience said: 'If you have any power of reasoning, you
must know that "knight", "king" and "conqueror" can refer
to one and the same person. It is good to be called a knight,
for men will kneel to him; it is better to be called a king, for
he has the power to create knights; but to be called a con-
queror—that results from special grace and from a valiant
heart, coupled with courtesy, by which he turns nobodies

To make lordes of laddes of londe þat he wynneth,
And fre men foule thralles þat folweth nou3t his lawes.
The Iuwes, þat were gentil-men, Iesu þei dispised,   [465
Bothe his lore and his lawe; now ar þei lowe cherlis.
As wyde as þe worlde is, wonyeth þere none
But vnder tribut and taillage, as tykes and cherles.
And þo þat bicome Crysten by conseille of þe Baptiste
Aren frankeleynes, fre men, þorw fullyng þat þei toke,   [470
And gentel-men with Iesu, for Iesus was yfolled,
And vppon Caluarye on crosse ycrouned kynge of Iewes.
    It bicometh to a kynge to kepe and to defende,
And conquerour of conquest his lawes and his large.
And so dide Iesus þe Iewes; he iustified and tau3te hem   [475
Þe lawe of lyf that last shal euere,
And fended fram foule yueles, feueres and fluxes,
And fro fendes þat in hem were, and fals bileue.
Þo was he Iesus of Iewes called, gentel prophete,
And kynge of her kyngdome and croune bar of þornes.   [480
And þo conquered he on crosse as conquerour noble;
My3t no deth hym fordo, ne adown brynge,
That he ne aros and regned and rauysshed helle.
And þo was he "conquerour" called of quikke and of ded,
For he 3af Adam and Eue and other mo blisse,   [485
Þat longe hadde leyne bifore as Lucyferes cherles.
And sith he 3af largely alle his lele lyges
Places in paradys at her partynge hennes,
He may wel be called "conquerour", and þat is Cryst to mene.
Ac þe cause þat he cometh þus with crosse of his passioun   [490
Is to wissen vs þerewyth, þat whan þat we ben tempted
Þerwith to fy3te and fenden vs fro fallyng into synne,
And se bi his sorwe þat whoso loueth ioye
To penaunce and to pouerte he moste putten hymseluen,
And moche wo in þis worlde willen and suffren.'. . .   [495

    Þus Conscience of Crist and of þe crosse carped,
And conseilled me to knele þerto; and þanne come, me thou3te,
One *spiritus paraclitus* to Pieres and to his felawes;
In lyknesse of a li3tnynge he ly3te on hem alle,
And made hem konne and knowe alkyn langages.   [500
I wondred what þat was, and wagged Conscience,
And was afered of the ly3te, for in fyres lyknesse

---

⁴⁷⁵ dide: MS ded   ⁴⁷⁸ were: MS was

into lords in the lands he conquers and free men who disobey his laws into miserable slaves. The Jews, who were of gentle stock, despised Jesus and His teaching and His law; now they are reduced to the level of peasants. Throughout the world, not one is exempt from paying tribute and taxes like yokels and labourers. But those who followed the advice of St John the Baptist and became Christians are franklins and free holders, by virtue of the baptism they received, sharing the freedom of gentle birth with Jesus, for Jesus was baptised and crowned King of the Jews upon the Cross on Calvary.

'It behoves a king and conqueror to preserve and defend his laws and be bountiful to those whom he has conquered; This was how Jesus behaved towards the Jews, to whom He brought justification, teaching them the law of everlasting life and defending them against loathsome diseases, such as fevers and fluxes, and against evil spirits that possessed them and false beliefs. Then the Jews called Him Jesus, noble prophet and king of their realm, and He wore the crown of thorns. Then He won victory on the cross, like a high-born conqueror. Death could not destroy Him or vanquish Him or prevent Him from rising again and reigning and despoiling hell. Then He was given the name of "conqueror" by the living and the dead, for He brought joy to Adam and Eve and many others who had for a long time before been in thrall to Lucifer, and since He unstintingly gave places in Paradise after death to His loyal servants, He may well be called "conqueror", that is to say, Christ.

'But the reason why He comes like this with the cross of His passion is to teach us thereby to use it as a weapon when we are tempted, to defend ourselves against falling into sin; and also to see from His sorrow that whoever desires joy must set himself to penance and poverty, and seek to endure much suffering in this world.'

Conscience talked to me thus about Christ and about the cross, and bade me kneel before it.

Then, it seemed to me, the Holy Ghost, the Paraclete, came to Piers and his companions, alighting on them all like lightning, and caused them to know and understand all manner of tongues. I wondered what that might be, and gave Conscience a nudge, being fearful of the light—for the Holy Paraclete hovered over them all in the likeness of fire.

Spiritus paraclitus ouer-spradde hem alle.
   Quod Conscience, and kneled, 'Þis is Crystes messager,
And cometh fro þe grete God, and Grace is his name.   [505
Knele now,' quod Conscience, 'and if þow canst synge,
Welcome hym and worshipe hym with "*veni, creator spiritus*".'
Thanne songe I þat songe and so did many hundreth,
And cryden with Conscience, 'Help vs, God of grace!'
And þanne bigan Grace to go with Piers Plowman,   [510
And conseilled hym and Conscience þe comune to sompne—
'For I wil dele to-daye and dyuyde grace,
To alkynnes creatures þat kan her fyue wittes,
Tresore to lyue by to her lyues ende,
And wepne to fyȝte with þat wil neure faille.   [515
For Antecryst and his al þe worlde shal greue,
And acombre þe, Conscience, but if Cryst þe helpe.
And fals prophetes fele, flatereres and glosers
Shullen come, and be curatoures ouer kynges and erlis,
And Pryde shal be pope prynce of holycherche.   [520
Coueytyse and Vnkyndenesse cardinales hym to lede.
Forþi,' quod Grace, 'er I go I wil gyue ȝow tresore,
And wepne to fiȝte with whan Antecryst ȝow assailleth.'
And gaf eche man a grace to gye with hymseluen,
That ydelnesse encombre hym nouȝt, envye, ne pryde,   [525
     Diuisiones graciarum sunt, etc.
   Some he ȝaf wytte with wordes to shewe,
Witte to wynne her lyflode with, as þe worlde asketh,
As prechoures and prestes and prentyces of lawe,
Þei lelly to lyue by laboure of tonge,
And bi witte to wissen other as Grace hem wolde teche.   [530
And some he kenned crafte and kunnynge of syȝte,
With sellyng and buggynge her bylyf to wynne,
And some he lered to laboure, a lele lyf and a trewe,
And somme he tauȝte to tilie, to dyche and to thecche,
To wynne with her lyflode by lore of his techynge.   [535
And some to dyuyne and diuide, noumbres to kenne;
And some to compas craftily and coloures to make;
And some to se and to saye what shulde bifalle,
Bothe of wel and of wo telle it or it felle,
As astronomyenes þorw astronomye and philosophres wyse.   [540
And some to ryde and to recoeure þat vnriȝtfully was wonne;
He wissed hem wynne it aȝeyne þorw wightnesse of handes,

---

528 prentyces: MS prentyce

Kneeling, Conscience said: 'This is Christ's messenger, who comes from Almighty God; His name is Grace. Fall on your knees and, if you know how to sing, greet Him and worship Him with the hymn: "Come, Holy Ghost [our souls inspire]".' Then I, and many hundreds more, sang that song, and joined in Conscience's cry of 'Help us, God of grace!'

Then Grace began to accompany Piers the Ploughman, and commanded him and Conscience to summon the people, saying: 'Today, to all men who have the use of their five senses I will distribute and apportion grace, a treasure to support them till the end of their lives and a never-failing weapon for combat. For Antichrist and his followers will harass the whole world and prove a hindrance to you, Conscience, unless Christ comes to your assistance. And many false prophets will come, flatterers and deceivers, and have charge of the souls of kings and nobles; and Pride will be Pope and head of Holy Church, with Covetousness and Uncharitableness as Cardinals to guide him. It is for this reason that, before I depart, I will give you treasure and a weapon to fight with when Antichrist assails you.'

He gave to every man a particular gift of grace by which to order his life, so that he should not be hindered by idleness, or envy, or pride; 'there are varieties of gifts, [but the same Spirit]'. To some He gave power of intellect, the gift of using words, intellectual skill by which to earn their necessary livelihood—preachers and priests and students of law, for example, must make an honest living by working with their tongues and use their intellect to instruct other people, as Grace may direct them.

Into some He instilled skill in trading and shrewdness of eye, to gain their livelihood by selling and buying; He taught some to live a faithful and honest life as labourers, and some to earn their living by tilling and ditching and thatching, as instructed by His teaching; some to explain and analyse and understand numbers, some to make skilful compass-measurements and fashion pigments, and some to perceive and say what would come about and foretell both joy and sorrow before they happened, as astronomers do by means of astronomy, and wise philosophers. He instructed some to take horse and recover what had been wrongfully seized, winning it back by the strength of their hands and wresting it from false dealers with rough and ready justice. To some He

And fecchen it fro fals men with Foluyles lawes.
And some he lered to lyue in longynge to ben hennes,
In pouerte and in penaunce to preye for alle Crystene.   [545
And alle he lered to be lele, and eche a crafte loue other,
And forbad hem alle debate þat none were amonge hem.
'Thowgh some be clenner þan somme, ʒe se wel', quod Grace,
'Þat he þat vseth þe fairest crafte, to þe foulest I couth haue put

                                                                      hym,
Þinketh alle', quod Grace, 'þat grace cometh of my ʒifte;   [550
Loke þat none lakke other, but loueth alle as bretheren.
And who þat moste maistries can, be myldest of berynge,
And crouneth Conscience kynge and maketh Crafte ʒowre stuward,
And after Craftes conseille clotheth ʒow and fede.
For I make Pieres þe Plowman my procuratour and my reve,   [555
And regystrere to receyue *redde quod debes*.
My prowor and my plowman Piers shal ben on erthe,
And for to tulye treuthe a teme shal he haue.'
    Grace gaue Piers a teme, foure gret oxen;
Þat on was Luke, a large beste and a lowe-chered,   [560
And Marke, and Mathew þe þrydde, myghty bestes bothe,
And ioigned to hem one Iohan, most gentil of alle,
Þe prys nete of Piers plow, passyng alle other.
    And Grace gaue Pieres, of his goodnesse, foure stottis,
Al þat his oxen eryed, þey to harwe after.   [565
On hyʒte Austyne and Ambrose another,
Gregori þe grete clerke and Ierome þe gode;
Þise foure, þe feithe to teche, folweth Pieres teme,
And harwed in an handwhile al holy scripture,
Wyth two harwes þat þei hadde, an olde and a newe,   [570
    Id est, vetus testamentum et nouum.
    And Grace gaue greynes, þe cardynales vertues,
And sewe hem in mannes soule and sithen he tolde her names.
Spiritus prudencie þe firste seed hyʒte,
And who so eet þat, ymagyne he shulde,
Ar he did any dede deuyse wel þe ende;   [575
And lerned men a ladel bugge with a longe stele,
Þat cast for to kepe a crokke to saue þe fatte abouen.
    The secounde seed hiʒte *spiritus temperancie.*
He þat ete of þat seed hadde suche a kynde,
Shulde neuere mete ne mochel drynke make hym to swelle,   [580
Ne sholde no scorner ne scolde oute of skyl hym brynge,

572 hem: MS it

taught a life of desire to leave this world, and of prayer, in poverty and penance, for all Christian souls. He taught that all must be faithful to their callings and that there must be loving-kindness between the different vocations, and forbade that there should be any strife among them.

'It must be apparent to you', said Grace, 'that, though some are cleaner than others, I could have set the man who has the cleanest tasks to do the dirtiest. Remember, all of you, that grace comes by my gift. See to it that none of you disparages another, but that you all love one another like brothers. Whoever has the greatest gifts must be the most unassuming in his bearing. Make Conscience your crowned king and Skill your steward, and clothe and feed yourselves in the light of Skill's teaching.

'I appoint Piers the Ploughman as my proctor and bailiff to receive as my agent "repayment of what you owe". Piers shall by my purveyor and my ploughman on earth, and he shall have a team to till the land with Truth.'

Grace gave Piers a team of four great oxen. The first was Luke, a large and mild-faced beast; then there was Mark, and Matthew the third—both of them powerful beasts—and, coupled with them, John, the most noble of all, the prize ox of Piers's ploughing team, which surpassed all the rest. In His goodness, Grace also gave Piers four bullocks to harrow all the land that had been ploughed by his oxen. One was called Augustine, and the second, Ambrose; also there was Gregory, the great scholar, and the holy Jerome. These four followed Piers's ox-team to teach the faith, and, in a hand's space of time, harrowed the whole of Holy Scripture with two harrows that they had, one old and one new, 'that is to say, the Old Testament and the New Testament.'

Grace also gave grains of corn, which were the Cardinal Virtues, to be sown in man's soul, and He proceeded to recite their names. The first seed was called 'the Spirit of Prudence'. Whoever ate that would reflect and consider the consequences before he embarked on any action; by it, whoever intended to watch a cooking-pot would be taught to buy a ladle with a long handle, so as to prevent the surface fat from boiling over.

The second seed was called 'the Spirit of Moderation'. Anyone who ate that seed was endowed with these qualities: he would never distend himself with eating or heavy drinking; neither mockery nor nagging would make him

Ne wynnynge, ne welthe of worldeliche ricchesse,
Waste worde of ydelnesse, ne wykked speche meue;
Shulde no curyous clothe comen on hys rugge,
Ne no mete in his mouth þat maister Iohan spiced.   [585
   The thridde seed þat Pieres sewe was *spiritus fortitudinis*.
And whoso eet of þat seed hardy was eure
To suffre al þat God sent, sykenesse and angres;
Myȝte no lesynge ne lyere ne losse of worldely catel
Maken hym for any mournynge, þat he nas merye in soule,   [590
And bolde and abydynge bismeres to suffre,
And playeth al with pacyence *et parce michi, domine*,
And couered hym vnder conseille of Catoun þe wyse;
    Esto forti animo, cum sis dampnatus inique.
   The fierthe seed þat Pieres sewe was *spiritus iusticie*,
And he þat eet of þat seed shulde be euere trewe   [595
With God, and nouȝt agast but of gyle one.
For gyle goth so pryuely þat good faith other-while
May nouȝte ben aspyed for *spiritus iusticie*.
Spiritus iusticie spareth nouȝte to spille
Hem þat ben gulty, and forto correcte   [600
Þe kynge, ȝif he falle in gylte or in trespasse.
For counteth he no kynges wratthe whan he in courte sitteth
To demen as a domes-man; adradde was he neure,
Noither of duke ne of deth, þat he ne dede þe lawe,
For present or for preyere or any prynces lettres;   [605
He dede equite to alle euene-forth his powere.
   Thise foure sedes Pieres sewe and sitthe he did hem harwe
Wyth olde lawe and newe lawe, þat loue myȝte wexe
Amonge þe foure vertues, and vices destroye.
For comunelich in contrees kammokes and wedes   [610
Fouleth þe fruite in þe felde, þere þei growe togyderes;
And so don vices vertues worthy.
Quod Piers: 'Harweth alle þat kunneth kynde witte bi conseille of
                              þis doctours,
And tulyeth after her techynge þe cardinale vertues.'
'Aȝeines þi greynes', quod Grace, 'bigynneth for to ripe,   [615
Ordeigne þe an hous, Piers to herberwe in þi cornes.'
'By God! Grace,' quod Piers, 'ȝe moten gyue tymbre,
And ordeyne þat hous ar ȝe hennes wende.'
And Grace gaue hym þe crosse, with þe croune of þornes,
That Cryst vpon Caluarye for mankynde on pyned,   [620

---

582 worldeliche: MS wordeliche   616 Piers: MS qd. Piers

unreasonable; he would remain unmoved by acquisitions or abundance of worldly wealth, by superfluous idle words or evil speaking; he would not put elaborate clothes on his back, or food flavoured with chef's spices into his mouth.

The third seed that Piers sowed was 'the Spirit of Fortitude'. Whoever ate that seed always endured courageously whatever sickness or afflictions God sent. Slanders, lies, loss of worldly goods were all powerless to prevent him, through grief, from being light of heart. He suffered calumnies bravely and steadfastly, taking pleasure in all through patience and the prayer 'Spare me, O Lord', and sheltered under the advice of wise Cato: 'Be strong in spirit, when you are unjustly condemned'.

The fourth seed that Piers sowed was 'the Spirit of Justice'. Anyone who ate that seed would always be true to God and frightened of nothing except deceit. For deceit goes to work so secretly that sometimes good faith cannot be recognised as 'the Spirit of Justice'. 'The Spirit of Justice' does not hesitate to punish the guilty and to correct the king himself, if he is culpable or at fault, for, when he sits in court as a judge to give his ruling. he takes no account of a king's anger. Neither fear of noblemen nor fear of death ever kept him from carrying out the law, bribes and petitions and royal letters notwithstanding. He dealt out justice to all, as far as it was within his power.

Piers sowed these four seeds and then had them harrowed by the Old Law and the New Law, so that love might spring up among the four virtues and destroy vices. For it frequently happens in the country that, where they grow side by side in the field, rest-harrow and weeds spoil the crops, and so do vices spoil good virtues.

Piers said: 'Harrow all the fruits of natural intelligence with the counsel of these Doctors of the Church, and till the Cardinal Virtues in accordance with their teaching!'

Grace said: 'Give orders for a house, Piers, in which to store your corn, in preparation for the time when your grain begins to ripen.'

Piers said: 'By God! Grace, before You depart, You must provide timber and give orders for the house!'

Grace gave him the cross on which Christ suffered for mankind on Calvary, and the crown of thorns, and, out of

And of his baptesme and blode þat he bledde on rode
He made a maner morter, and Mercy it hiȝte.
And þerewith Grace bigan to make a good foundement,
And watteled it and walled it with his peynes and his passioun,
And of al holywrit he made a rofe after,   [625
And called þat hous Vnite, holicherche on Englisshe.
And whan þis dede was done, Grace deuised
A carte, hyȝte Cristendome, to carye Pieres sheues;
And gaf hym caples to his carte, Contricioun and Confessioun,
And made Presthode haywarde, þe while hymself went   [630
As wyde as þ worlde is, with Pieres to tulye treuthe.

   Now is Pieres to þe plow, and Pruyde it aspyde,
And gadered hym a grete oest; to greuen he þinketh
Conscience and al Crystene and cardinale vertues,
Blowe hem doune and breke hem and bite atwo þe mores;   [635
And sente forth Surquydous, his seriaunt of armes,
And his spye Spille-loue, one Speke-yuel-byhynde.
Þise two come to Conscience and to Crystene peple,
And tolde hem tydynges, 'þat tyne thei shulde the sedes,
That Pieres þere hadde ysowen, þe cardynal vertues;   [640
And Pieres berne worth broke; and þei þat ben in Vnite
Shulle come out, and Conscience and ȝowre two caples,
Confessioun and Contricioun, and ȝowre carte, þe Byleue
Shal be coloured so queyntly and keuered vnder owre sophistrie,
Þat Conscience shal nouȝte knowe by contricioun   [645
Ne by confessioun, who is Cristene or hethen,
Ne no maner marchaunt þat with moneye deleth,
Where he wynne wyth riȝte, with wronge, or with vsure.
With suche coloures and queyntise cometh Pryde y-armed,
With þe lorde þat lyueth after þe luste of his body,   [650
To wasten, on welfare and on wykked kepynge,
Al þe worlde in a while þorw owre witte', quod Pruyde.

   Quod Conscience to alle Crystene þo: 'My conseille is to wende
Hastiliche into Vnyte, and holde we vs þere,
And preye we þat a pees were in Piers berne þe Plowman.   [655
For witterly I wote wel we beth nouȝte of strengthe
To gone agayne Pryde, but Grace were with vs.'
And þanne cam Kynde Wytte Conscience to teche,
And cryde and comaunded al Crystene peple,
For to deluen a dyche depe aboute Vnite,   [660
That holycherche stode in Vnite, as it a pyle were.

645 Conscience: MS conscioun   661 were supplied

Christ's baptism and the blood that He shed on the cross, He made a kind of mortar called Mercy. With this, Grace set about making a good foundation, and wattled and walled it with Christ's sufferings and passion, then made a roof of the whole of Holy Scripture, and called that house Unity, or, as we say in English, Holy Church. When this was completed, Grace designed a cart, called Christendom, to carry Piers's sheaves, and gave him horses, called Contrition and Confession, to draw his cart, and made Priesthood the hay-ward, what time He himself went the whole breadth of the world with Piers to till the crop of Truth.

Then Piers set himself to the plough. Pride saw what was happening and gathered to himself a great host, thinking to bring trouble on Conscience and all Christian people, and the Cardinal Virtues, blowing them down and shattering them, and snapping the roots asunder. He dispatched his sergeant-at-arms, Arrogance, and his spy, Destroy-Love, that is, Speak-evil-behind-a-man's-back. These two came to Conscience and to the assembly of Christians and told them these tidings: they would lose the seeds of the Cardinal Virtues which Piers had sown there. They added: 'Piers's barn shall be broken open, and those who are inside Unity shall come out, and Conscience and your two horses, Confession and Contrition, and your cart, the Creed, shall be so cunningly disguised and hidden beneath your sophistries that Conscience will be unable to tell, by means of either contrition or confession, who is Christian or who is heathen. Nor will he be able to tell whether any merchant who handles money is making his profits by right means, by wrong means, or by usury. Pride, accompanied by the lord who lives according to his fleshly desires, comes armed in subtle disguises such as these, to lay the whole world waste soon with high living and evil modes of life, under our guidance.' These were the words of Pride.

Then Conscience said to all Christian people: 'My advice is that we should hurry into Unity and stay there, and pray that there may be peace within the barn of Piers the Ploughman, for, indeed, I am well aware that we have no power to counter Pride unless Grace be with us.'

Then Natural Intelligence came to instruct Conscience, crying out the command to all Christian people to dig a deep ditch round about Unity, so that Holy Church should stand on Unity as, so to speak, on a firm foundation.

K

Conscience comaunded þo al Crystene to delue,
And make a muche mote, þat myȝte ben a strengthe,
To helpe holycherche and hem þat it kepeth.
Thanne alkyn Crystene, saue comune wommen,   [665
Repenteden and refused synne, saue they one;
And fals men, flatereres, vsureres and theues,
Lyeres and questmongeres, þat were forsworen ofte,
Wytynge and willefully with þe false helden,
And for syluer were forswore, sothely þei wist it.   [670
Þere nas no Crystene creature þat kynde witte hadde,
Saue schrewes one, suche as I spak of,
That he ne halpe a quantite holynesse to wexe.
Somme þorw bedes-byddynge and somme þorw pylgrymage,
And other pryue penaunce, and some þorw penyes-delynge.   [675
And þanne welled water for wikked werkes,
Egerlich ernynge out of mennes eyen.
Clennesse of þe comune and clerkes clene lyuynge
Made Vnite holicherche in holynesse to stonde.
'I care nouȝte,' quod Conscience, 'þough Pryde come nouthe, [680
Þe lorde of luste shal be letted al þis Lente, I hope.
Cometh', quod Conscience, 'ȝe Cristene, and dyneth,
Þat han laboured lelly al þis Lente-tyme.
Here is bred yblessed, and Goddes body þervnder.
Grace þorw Goddes worde gaue Pieres power   [685
And myȝtes to maken it, and men to ete it after,
In helpe of her hele onys in a moneth,
Or as ofte as þey hadden nede, þo þat hadde ypayed
To Pieres pardoun þe Plowman *redde quod debes*.'
'How?' quod al þe comune, 'þow conseillest vs to ȝelde   [690
Al þat we owen any wyȝte ar we go to housel?'
'That is my conseille,' quod Conscience, 'and cardynale vertues,
Þat vche man forȝyue other, and þat wyl þe *paternoster*,
     Et dimitte nobis debita nostra, etc.,
And so to ben assoilled and sithen ben houseled.'
'ȝe, bawe!' quod a brewere, 'I wil nouȝt be reuled,   [695
Bi Iesu! for al ȝowre ianglynge, with *spiritus iusticie*,
Ne after Conscience, by Cryste! whil I can selle
Bothe dregges and draffe and drawe it at on hole
Þikke ale and þinne ale, for þat is my kynde,
And nouȝte hakke after holynesse; holde þi tonge, Conscience! [700
Of *spiritus iusticie* þow spekest moche an ydel!'

---

667 flatereres: MS flateres   686 And *supplied*

Then Conscience ordered all Christians to dig and make a great moat as a strong defence which would help Holy Church and its guardians. At this, Christians in all walks of life repented and turned against sin. The only exceptions were women of the streets and men who lived by falsehood: flatterers, usurers, thieves, liars, and professional holders of judicial enquiries who regularly perjured themselves, upheld false claims wittingly and deliberately and, with full knowledge, were forsworn in return for bribes. Apart from such wretched creatures as these, there was not one Christian in possession of his faculties that did not help the increase of some measure of holiness, some by means of prayer, some by pilgrimage, others by secret penance and some by almsgiving. Then bitter tears for sin welled up and flowed from men's eyes. The purity of the mass of the people and the clean lives of the clergy established Unity-Holy Church in holiness.

'I do not care if Pride does come now', said Conscience. 'The Lord Lust will, I trust, be thwarted for the whole of this Lent. You Christian people who have toiled faithfully throughout this Lenten season, come and dine! Here is blessed bread and God's Body under the form of it. By the Word of God, Grace gave to Piers the power and ability to make it, and to men the subsequent eating of it as a help to their salvation once a month, or as often as they needed—those of them who had paid their dues in accordance with the Pardon of Piers the Ploughman, "Repay what you owe".'

'What?' said all the people. 'You are telling us to pay back all that we owe to anyone before we go to Communion?'

'That is my advice, and the advice of the Cardinal Virtues,' said Conscience, 'namely, that all men should forgive one another, as the Lord's Prayer requires: "And forgive us our trespasses, as we forgive them that trespass against us", and then be absolved and, after that, make their Communion.'

'Be damned to that for a tale!' said a brewer. 'Never mind all your patter; by the Lord Christ! I will not be ruled by "the Spirit of Justice" or by Conscience, so long as I can sell dregs and pigswill, and draw strong ale and watery ale out of the same bunghole. That is *my* nature, not grubbing around after holiness. Hold your tongue, Conscience! You are wasting your breath with all this talk of "the Spirit of Justice".'

'You, brewer, are a miserable, cursed wretch, past saving, unless God helps you', said Conscience. 'If you do not live

'Caytyue,' quod Conscience, 'cursed wrecche!
Vnblessed artow, brewere, but if þe God helpe;
But þow lyue by lore of *spiritus iusticie*,
Þe chief seed þat Pieres sewe, y-saued worstow neuere.   [705
But Conscience þe comune fede, and cardynale vertues,
Leue it wel, þei ben loste bothe lyf and soule.'
'Thanne is many man ylost', quod a lewed vycory,
'I am a curatour of holykyrke, and come neure in my tyme
Man to me, þat me couth telle of cardinale vertues,   [710
Or þat acounted Conscience at a cokkes fether or an hennes!
I knewe neure cardynal þat he ne cam fro þe pope,
And we clerkes, whan þey come, for her comunes payeth,
For her pelure and her palfreyes mete and piloures þat hem
                                                      folweth.

Þe comune *clamat cotidie* eche a man to other,   [715
"Þe contre is þe curseder þat cardynales come inne;
And þere they ligge and lenge moste, lecherye þere regneth".
Forþi,' quod þis vicori, 'be verrey God, I wolde
That no cardynal come amonge þe comune peple,
But in her holynesse holden hem stille   [720
At Auynoun, amonge þe Iuwes, *cum sancto sanctus eris, etc.*,
Or in Rome, as here rule wole, þe reliques to kepe;
And þow, Conscience, in kynges courte, and shuldest neure come
                                                      þennes,

And Grace, þat þow gredest so of, gyour of alle clerkes,
And Pieres with his newe plow and eke with his olde,   [725
Emperour of al the worlde, þat alle men were Cristene!
Inparfyt is þat pope þat al peple shulde helpe,
And sendeth hem þat sleeth suche as he shulde saue;
And wel worth Piers þe Plowman, þat pursueth God in doynge,
Qui pluit super iustos et iniustos at ones,   [730
And sent þe sonne to saue a cursed mannes tilthe,
As bryȝte as to þe best man and to þe beste woman.
Riȝte so Pieres þe Plowman peyneth hym to tulye
As wel for a wastour and wenches of þe stuwes,
As for hymself and his seruauntz, saue he is firste yserued;   [735
And trauailleth and tulyeth for a tretour also sore
As for a trewe tydy man al tymes ylyke.
And worshiped be he þat wrouȝte al, bothe good and wykke,
And suffreth þat synful be, til some tyme þat þei repente.
And God amende þe pope, þat pileth holykirke,   [740

---

729 pursueth: MS sueth

according to the teaching of "the Spirit of Justice", the prin-
cipal seed which Piers sowed, you will never know salvation.
Unless Conscience and the Cardinal Virtues feed the people,
rest assured, they will be damned in body and soul.'

'In that case, many a man is doomed to damnation', said a
vicar of little learning. 'I am a priest of Holy Church, charged
with the care of souls, but, in all my life, no one ever ap-
proached me who could tell me about Cardinal Virtues, or
who rated Conscience at the value of a cock's or hen's feather.
The only "Cardinals" I ever knew came from the Pope, and,
when they come, we clergy have to pay for their keep, and
for their furred clothes, and for food for their horses, and for
their train of robbers. Every day, the people complain to
one another: "The land that Cardinals enter is the more accursed
for it, and lechery holds the greatest sway wherever they
lodge and dwell".

'So,' this vicar went on, 'by the true God! I wish that
Cardinals would not come visiting the people but stay at
home and preserve their holy state at Avignon, among the
Jews ("with the loyal thou dost show thyself loyal", as the
Psalm says), or else in Rome, guarding the relics in accordance
with their Rule. As for you, Conscience, you should remain
in the king's court and never leave it, and Grace, that you
make so much clamour about, should act as guide to all the
clergy, and Piers, with his new and his old plough, should be
emperor over all the world, so that all men might become
Christians.

'Perfection is lacking in the Pope who ought to help all
men, but sends out those who destroy the very people that it
is his duty to save. Blessed be Piers the Ploughman, who, in
his actions, is a follower of God who "sends rain on the just
and on the unjust" alike and makes the sun shine as brightly
to save a wicked man's crops as He makes it shine on the best
of men and women! In just the same way Piers the Ploughman
labours as hard in the fields for wastrels and prostitutes as he
does for himself and his servants (except that he takes the
first serving), and at all times puts as much toil into working
and cultivating the land for a traitor as for an honest, diligent
man.

'Glory be to Him who made all men, good and evil alike,
and is willing to let men continue in their sins until such time
as they repent! And God grant amendment to the Pope, who
pillages Holy Church and claims precedence over the king as

And cleymeth bifor þe kynge to be keper ouer Crystene,
And counteth nouȝt þough Crystene ben culled and robbed,
And fynt folke to fyȝte and Cristene blode to spille,
Aȝeyne þe olde lawe and newe lawe, as Luke þerof witnesseth,
    Non occides: michi vindictam, etc.'. . .

   Anon I felle aslepe,   [745
And mette ful merueillously þat, in mannes forme,
Antecryst cam þanne and al þe croppe of treuthe
Torned it vp-so-doune, and ouertilte þe rote,
And made fals sprynge and sprede and spede mennes nedes;
In eche a contre þere he cam, he cutte awey treuthe,   [750
And gert gyle growe þere, as he a god were.
Freres folwed þat fende, for he ȝaf hem copes,
And religiouse reuerenced hym and rongen here belles,
And al þe couent forth cam to welcome þat tyraunt
And alle hise, as wel as hym, saue onlich folis;   [755
Which folis were wel leuer to deye þan to lyue
Lengore, sith leute was so rebuked.
And a fals fende Antecriste ouer alle folke regned;
And þat were mylde men and holy, þat no myschief dredden,
Defyed al falsenesse and folke þat it vsed;   [760
And what kynge þat hem conforted, knowynge hem any while,
They cursed, and her conseille, were it clerke or lewed.
   Antecriste hadde thus sone hundredes at his banere,
And Pryde it bare boldely aboute,
With a lorde þat lyueth after lykynge of body,   [765
That cam aȝein Conscience, þat kepere was and gyoure
Ouer kynde Crystene and cardynale vertues.
'I conseille,' quod Conscience þo, 'cometh with me, ȝe foles,
Into Vnyte holycherche and holde we vs there,
And crye we to Kynde, þat he come and defende vs,   [770
Foles, fro þis fendes lymes, for Piers loue þe Plowman.
And crye we to alle þe comune þat þei come to Vnite,
And þere abide and bikere aȝein Beliales children.'
   Kynd Conscience þo herde and cam out of þe planetes,
And sent forth his foreioures, feures and fluxes,   [775
Coughes and cardiacles, crampes and tothaches,
Rewmes, and radegoundes and roynouse scalles,
Byles and bocches and brennyng agues,
Frenesyes and foule yueles, forageres of kynde,

749 made *supplied*   757 leute: MS lenten

a protector of Christian men, but does not care if Christians are killed and robbed, and provides people to fight and spill Christian blood, in contravention of both the Old Law and the New Law, as St Luke bears witness: "Do not kill"; "Vengeance is mine [I will repay]".'

Straightway I fell asleep, and dreamed a most strange dream, in which Antichrist came, in the form of a man, and toppled all Truth's crop upside down, upturning the roots, and caused Falsehood to spring up and spread and further men's needs. Wherever he went he hacked away truth and made deceit grow in its place, as if he had divine right. Friars became that devil's followers, because he provided them with copes; the religious Orders paid him homage and rang their bells, and the whole religious community came out to welcome that tyrant and all his supporters as well, except only those who, in the foolishness of their simplicity, much preferred to die rather than to continue to live, since loyal faith was so abused and the false fiend Antichrist reigned over everyone. They were gentle, holy men, who feared no misfortune. They defied falsehood of every kind and those who employed it, and cursed any king who gave them support or acknowledged them for any length of time and members of their council, whether clergy or laity.

So in a short time Antichrist had hundreds under his banner and Pride swaggered about carrying it, together with a lord who lives according to the pleasures of the flesh, who advanced against Conscience, the guardian and guide of Christian people and the Cardinal Virtues.

'My advice to you who keep the foolishness of simplicity', said Conscience, 'is to come with me into Unity, that is Holy Church, and stay there, and beseech Nature to come and defend us, the foolish simple, from these limbs of the devil for the love of Piers the Ploughman. Let us also beseech all the people to come to Unity and remain there and contend against the children of Belial.'

Then Nature heard Conscience and came forth from the planets. He sent out his foragers: fevers and discharges, coughs and heart-spasms, cramps and toothaches, colds and sores in the eyes, scabby eczema, boils, swellings and burning agues, frenzies and horrible diseases. These foragers of Nature

Hadde yprykked and prayed polles of peple,   [780
Þat largelich a legioun lese her lyf sone.
There was—'harrow and help! here cometh Kynde,
With Deth þat is dredful, to vndone vs alle!'
The lorde that lyued after lust tho alowde cryde
After Conforte, a knyghte, to come and bere his banere.   [785
'Alarme! alarme!' quod þat lorde, 'eche lyf kepe his owne!'
And þanne mette þis men ar mynstralles myȝte pipe,
And ar heraudes of armes hadden descreued lordes.
   Elde þe hore he was in þe vauntwarde,
And bare þe banere bifor Deth, by riȝte he it claymed.   [790
Kynde come after with many kene sores,
As pokkes and pestilences, and moche poeple shente;
So Kynde þorw corupciouns kulled ful manye.
Deth cam dryuende after and al to doust passhed
Kynges and knyȝtes, kayseres and popes;   [795
Lered ne lewed, he let no man stonde,
That he hitte euene þat euere stired after.
Many a louely lady and lemmanes of knyghtes
Swouned and swelted for sorwe of Dethes dyntes.
   Conscience of his curteisye to Kynde he bisouȝte   [800
To cesse and suffre, and see where þei wolde
Leue Pryde pryuely and be parfite Cristene.
And Kynde cessed tho, to se þe peple amende.
Fortune gan flateren thenne þo fewe þat were alyue,
And byhight hem longe lyf, and Lecherye he sent   [805
Amonges al manere men, wedded and vnwedded,
And gadered a gret hoste al agayne Conscience.
This Lecherye leyde on with a laughyng chiere,
And with pryue speche and peynted wordes,
And armed hym in ydelnesse and in hiegh berynge.   [810
He bare a bowe in his hande and manye blody arwes,
Weren fethered with fair biheste and many a false truthe.
With his vntydy tales he tened ful ofte
Conscience and his compaignye, of holicherche þe techeres.
   Thanne cam Coueityse, and caste how he myȝte   [815
Ouercome Conscience and cardynal vertues,
And armed hym in auaryce and hungriliche lyued.
His wepne was al wiles to wynnen and to hyden;
With glosynges and with gabbynges he gyled þe peple.
Symonye hym sent to assaille Conscience,   [820

---

813 With: MS Wit.

pierced and preyed upon men's heads so that fully a legion died straightway. There were cries of:

'Alas! Help! Here comes Nature, along with Death the terrible, to destroy us all!'

The lord who lived by lust then called loudly for a knight, Comfort, to come and carry his banner saying: 'To arms! To arms! Every man for himself!' Then these men came face to face before minstrels could blow their pipes and before the heralds-of-arms had proclaimed the names of the knights.

Hoary-headed Old Age was in the van and carried the banner in front of Death, claiming it as his right. Nature followed with many grievous diseases, such as smallpox and the plague, and destroyed great numbers, killing many by illnesses. Death came rushing in his wake and pounded kings and knights, emperors and popes to dust, leaving no one, cleric or layman, standing. Those that he hit squarely never moved again. Many a lovely lady and many a knight's sweetheart swooned away and died through the pain of death's blows.

Out of compassion, Conscience begged Nature to stay his hand and wait and see whether they would quietly leave Pride and become true Christians. Nature then desisted, in order to observe the people's amendment.

Then Fortune fawned on those few who were left alive. He promised them long life, and sent Lechery among men of every condition, married and single, and mustered a great host against Conscience. Lechery set to work with a laughing countenance and intimate whispers and flattering words, arming himself in idleness and arrogant bearing. He carried a bow in his hand and many bloodstained arrows feathered with fair promises and many spurious betrothals. He caused much vexation to Conscience and his companions, the teachers of Holy Church, with his unseemly tales.

Next came Covetousness, who cast about how he could overcome Conscience and the Cardinal Virtues. He armed himself in avarice and stinted himself of food. His weapon was every trick by which to gain possessions and hide them away; he deluded the people with deceits and lies. Simony sent him to attack Conscience, and preached to the people. They set up

And preched to þe peple, and prelates þei hem maden,
To holden with Antecryste, her temperaltes to saue;
And come to þe kynges conseille as a kene baroun,
And kneled to Conscience in courte afor hem alle,
And gart Gode-Feith flee and Fals to abide,   [825
And boldeliche bar adown with many a briȝte noble
Moche of þe witte and wisdome of Westmynster halle.
He iugged til a Iustice and iusted in his ere,
And ouertilte al his treuthe with 'take-þis-vp-amendement'.
And to þe arches in haste he ȝede anone after,   [830
And torned Ciuile into symonye, and sitthe he toke þe official;
For a mantel of menyuere, he made lele matrimonye
Departen ar deth cam and deuors shupte.
    'Allas!' quod Conscience, and cried þo, 'Wolde Criste, of his grace,
That Coueityse were Cristene, þat is so kene a fiȝter,   [835
And bolde and bidyng while his bagge lasteth!'
And þanne lowgh Lyf and leet dagge his clothes,
And armed hym in haste in harlotes wordes,
And helde Holynesse a iape and Hendenesse a wastour,
And lete Leute a cherle and Lyer a fre man;   [840
Conscience and conseille he counted it a folye.
Thus relyed Lyf for a litel fortune,
And pryked forth with Pryde, preyseth he no vertue,
Ne careth nouȝte how Kynde slow and shal come atte laste,
And culle alle erthely creatures saue Conscience one.   [845
Lyf leep asyde and lauȝte hym a lemman,
'Heel and I', quod he, 'and hieghnesse of herte
Shal do þe nouȝte drede noyther Deth ne Elde,
And to forȝete sorwe and ȝyue nouȝte of synne.'
This lyked Lyf and his lemman Fortune,   [850
And geten in her glorie a gadelyng atte laste,
One þat moche wo wrouȝte, Sleuthe was his name.
Sleuthe wex wonder ȝerne and sone was of age,
And wedded one Wanhope, a wenche of þe stuwes;
Her syre was a sysour þat neure swore treuthe,   [855
One Thomme two-tonge ateynte at vch a queste.
This Sleuthe was war of werre and a slynge made,
And threwe drede of dyspayre a dozein myle aboute.
For care Conscience þo cryed vpon Elde,
And bad hym fonde to fyȝte and afere Wanhope.   [860
    And Elde hent good hope and hastilich he shifte hym,

832 mantel: MS mentel   844 Ne: MS A   845 creatures: MS creature

prelates who would side with Antichrist in order to preserve their temporalities. He came to the king's council in the guise of a bold baron and went on his knees to Conscience in the court in front of everybody. He caused Good Faith to flee and Falsehood to remain, and boldly thrust down much of the sense and wisdom in the hall of Westminster with an abundance of shining coins. He trotted up to a judge and made a thrust at his ear, and overturned all his regard for truth with the words 'Take this, in return for an amendment'. Then he at once hurried off to the Court of Arches and turned Civil Law into simony, subsequently bribing the court officer. In return for a fur mantle, he caused true marriage to be severed before death, and arranged a divorce.

Then Conscience cried: 'Alas! Would to Christ that, by His grace, Covetousness were a Christian! He is such a keen warrior, bold and tenacious, as long as his purse lasts.'

Then Life laughed, and had his clothes cut with fashionable slits. He quickly armed himself in ribald words; he regarded Holiness as a joke and Courtesy as a spendthrift and considered Loyalty a bondsman and Liar a freeman; he reckoned Conscience and good advice as foolishness. So, as the result of a little good fortune, Life took courage again and rode on his way with Pride, esteeming no virtues, heedless of the slaughter wrought by Nature who, in the end, will come and kill all creatures on earth, save only Conscience.

Life leapt aside and snatched a paramour for himself, saying: 'Health and I and soaring spirits will make you fear neither Death nor Old Age, and forget sorrow and care nothing for sin.'

This pleased Life and Fortune, his mistress, and in their glorying they finally begot a vagabond called Sloth, who was the cause of many troubles. Sloth grew amazingly fast and soon came of age. He married Despair, a woman from the brothels. Her father was a juror, Tom Double-tongue, who never swore a true oath and was accused at every inquest. Sloth, being wary in combat, made a sling and hurled the fear of despair a dozen miles round about. Then Conscience in distress cried out to Old Age and besought him to try and fight and strike fear into Despair.

Old Age took good heart and quickly stirred himself, drove

And wayued awey Wanhope and with Lyf he fyȝteth.
And Lyf fleigh for fere to Fysyke after helpe,
And bisouȝte hym of socoure, and of his salue hadde,
And gaf hym golde, good woon þat gladded his herte,   [865
And þei gyuen hym agayne a glasen houve.
Lyf leued þat lechecrafte lette shulde Elde,
And dryuen awey Deth with dyas and dragges.

   And Elde auntred hym on Lyf, and atte laste he hitte
A fisicien with a forred hood, þat he fel in a palsye,   [870
And þere deyed þat doctour ar thre dayes after.
'Now I see', seyde Lyf, 'þat surgerye ne fisyke
May nouȝte a myte auaille to medle aȝein Elde.'
And in hope of his hele, gode herte he hente,
And rode so to Reuel, a ryche place and a merye;   [875
The companye of conforte, men cleped it sumtyme.
And Elde anone after me and ouer myne heed ȝede,
And made me balled bifore and bare on þe croune,
So harde he ȝede ouer myn hed, it wil be seen eure.
'Sire euel-ytauȝte Elde,' quod I, 'vnhende go with the!   [880
Sith whanne was þe way ouer mennes hedes?
Haddestow be hende,' quod I, 'þow woldest haue asked leue!'
'Ȝe! leue lordeyne!' quod he, and leyde on me with age,
And hitte me vnder þe ere, vnethe may ich here;
He buffeted me aboute þe mouthe and bette out my tethe,   [885
And gyued me in goutes, I may nouȝte go at large.
And of þe wo þat I was in my wyf had reuthe,
And wisshed ful witterly þat I were in heuene.
For þe lyme þat she loued me fore and leef was to fele,
On nyȝtes namely, whan we naked were,   [890
I ne myght in no manere maken it at hir wille,
So Elde and she sothly hadden it forbeten.

   And as I seet in þis sorwe I say how Kynde passed,
And Deth drowgh niegh me; for drede gan I quake,
And cried to Kynde out of care me brynge.   [895
'Loo! Elde þe hoore hath me biseye,
Awreke me, if ȝowre wille be, for I wolde ben hennes.'
'Ȝif þow wilt ben ywroken, wende into Vnite,
And holde þe þere eure tyl I sende for þe,
And loke þow conne somme crafte ar þow come þennes.'   [900
'Conseille me, Kynde,' quod I, 'what crafte is best to lerne?'
'Lerne to loue,' quod Kynde, 'and leue of alle othre.'

881 mennes: MS men   885 bette: MS bett

Despair away and fought against Life. Life fled in fear to Medicine for help, begging for his assistance, and obtained some of his ointment, paying him lavishly, which rejoiced his heart. In return, the physicians gave him a glass cap. Life believed that medical skill would prevent Old Age and drive Death away with remedies and drugs. Old Age pitted himself against Life and at last he struck a physician in a furred hood, causing him to be seized with palsy. Less than three days afterwards, that doctor died.

'I see now', said Life, 'that neither surgery nor medicine is of the slightest help in combating Old Age.'

He plucked up his courage and, hoping for health, rode off to Revelry—a rich, cheerful place, sometimes called 'comforting company'.

Thereupon Old Age came after me and passed over my head, making me bald in front and bare on top; he went over my head with such force that the signs will be permanent.

'Bad manners go with you, badly taught Sir Old Age!' I said. 'Since when did the way lie over men's heads? If you had had any courtesy, you would have asked permission.'

'Indeed? You precious vagabond!' he said, and set about me with Age, striking me under the ear so that I can hardly hear, buffeting me around the mouth and knocking out my teeth and laming me with gout so that I cannot walk abroad. My wife felt pity for the afflictions I suffered and heartily wished me in heaven, for I could not by any means make, at her desire, the limb for which she loved me and delighted to feel, especially at night, when we were naked, so completely had she and Old Age enfeebled it.

As I sat in this misery I saw how Nature passed by and Death approached me. I trembled with fear and called upon Nature to bring me out of sorrow:

'See, hoary Old Age has visited me! Avenge me, if you are willing, for I desire to go hence!'

'If you wish to be avenged, make your way into Unity and stay there permanently until I send for you, and see that you learn some craft before you leave.'

'Give me your advice, Nature. Which is the best craft to learn?' I said.

'Learn to love,' said Nature, 'and forsake everything else!'

'How shal I come to catel so, to clothe me and to fede?'
'And þow loue lelly,' quod he, 'lakke shal þe neure
Mete ne worldly wede whil þi lyf lasteth.'   [905
And þere, by conseille of Kynde, I comsed to rowme
Thorw Contricioun and Confessioun tyl I cam to Vnite;
And þere was Conscience constable, Cristene to saue,
And biseged sothly with seuene grete gyauntz
þat with Antecrist helden hard aȝein Conscience. . . .   [910

   Enuye herfore hated Conscience,
And freres to philosofye he fonde hem to scole,
The while Coueytise and Vnkyndenesse Conscience assailled.
In Vnite holycherche Conscience helde hym
And made Pees porter to pynne þe ȝates   [915
Of alle taletellers and tyterers in ydel.
Ypocrisye and he an hard saut þei made.
Ypocrysie atte ȝate hard gan fiȝte,
And wounded wel wykkedly many a wise techer,
þat with Conscience acorded and cardinale vertues.   [920
Conscience called a leche þat coude wel shryue;
'Go salue þo þat syke ben and þorw synne y-wounded.'
Shrifte shope sharpe salue and made men do penaunce
For her mysdedes þat þei wrouȝte hadden,
And þat Piers were payed *redde quod debes*.   [925
   Somme lyked nouȝte þis leche, and lettres þei sent,
Ȝif any surgien were in þe sege þat softer couth plastre.
Sire Lief-to-lyue-in-leccherye lay þere and groned;
For fastyng of a Fryday he ferde as he wolde deye.
'Ther is a surgiene in þis sege þat softe can handle,   [930
And more of phisyke bi fer and fairer he plastreth;
One frere Flaterere is phisiciene and surgiene',
Quod Contricioun to Conscience; 'Do hym come to Vnyte,
For here is many a man herte þorw Ypocrisie.'
'We han no nede,' quod Conscience, 'I wote no better leche   [935
Than persoun or parissh prest, penytancere or bisshop,
Saue Piers þe Plowman, þat hath powere ouer hem alle
And indulgence may do, but if dette lette it.
I may wel suffre,' seyde Conscience, 'syn ȝe desiren,
That frere Flaterer be fette and phisike ȝow syke.'   [940
   The frere herof herde, and hyed faste

---

905 worldly: MS wordly   919 a *supplied*   922 and *supplied*
927 in *supplied*   930 softe: MS soft

'How shall I by that means acquire money to clothe and feed myself?'

'If you love faithfully,' he said, 'you will never lack food or earthly clothing all the days of your life.'

Then, following Nature's advice, I began to journey through Contrition and Confession until I came to Unity. Conscience was in charge there, to keep Christians safe, besieged by seven great giants who fought hard against Conscience on the side of Antichrist.

Envy hated Conscience on this account, and set the friars to study philosophy, while Covetousness and Lack-of-natural-affection assailed Conscience. Conscience stayed firmly within Unity-Holy Church and set Peace as the doorkeeper to bar the gates against all tale-tellers and irresponsible tattlers. They and Hypocrisy made a fierce assault; Hypocrisy fought hard at the gate and grievously wounded many wise teachers who were on the side of Conscience and the Cardinal Virtues. Conscience summoned a doctor well versed in hearing confessions, saying: 'Go and heal those who are sick and wounded by sin!' Shrift concocted a stinging ointment and made people do penance for the sins which they had committed, and ensured that Piers's terms were satisfied: 'Pay back what you owe!'

Some people disliked this doctor and sent letters enquiring whether there was any surgeon in the place who could apply a less painful plaster. Sir Rejoicing-to-live-in-lechery lay there groaning, behaving as if he would die if he had to fast on Fridays. Contrition said to Conscience: 'There is a gentle-handed surgeon here, who knows far more about medicine and puts on more acceptable plasters. His name is Friar Flatterer, physician and surgeon. Summon him to Unity, for many people here have been wounded by Hypocrisy.'

'We have no need to', said Conscience. 'I know of no better doctor than the parson or the parish priest, the confessor or the bishop—except for Piers the Ploughman, who holds sway over all of them and may grant an indulgence, unless debt prevents it.'

He added: 'Since you desire it, I am willing to allow Friar Flatterer to be brought to dose those of you who are sick.'

The friar heard of this and speedily hurried off to a lord for a letter giving him leave to have charge of souls as if he were a parish priest. He boldly approached the bishop with his

To a lorde for a lettre, leue to haue to curen
As a curatour he were and cam with his lettres
Baldly to þe bisshop and his brief hadde,
In contrees þere he come in confessiouns to here;   [945
And cam þere Conscience was and knokked atte ȝate.
Pees vnpynned it, was porter of Vnyte,
And in haste asked what his wille were.
'In faith,' quod þis frere, 'for profit and for helthe
Carpe I wolde with Contricioun, and þerfore come I hider.'   [950
'He is sike,' seide Pees, 'and so ar many other;
Ypocrisie hath herte hem, ful harde is if þei keure.'
'I am a surgien,' seide þe segge, 'and salues can make;
Conscience knoweth me wel and what I can do bothe.'
'I preye þe,' quod Pees þo, 'ar þow passe ferther,   [955
What hattestow? I preye þe hele nouȝte þi name.'
'Certes,' seyde his felow, 'sire Penetrans-domos.'
'Ȝe, go þi gate,' quod Pees, 'bi God, for al þi phisyk,
But þow conne somme crafte, þow comest nouȝt herinne!
I knewe such one ones, nouȝte eighte wynter passed,   [960
Come in þus ycoped at a courte þere I dwelt,
And was my lordes leche and my ladyes bothe.
And at þe last þis limitour, þo my lorde was out,
He salued so owre wommen til somme were with childe!'
Hende-speche het Pees opene þe ȝates—   [965
'Late in þe frere and his felawe and make hem faire chere.
He may se and here, so it may bifalle,
That Lyf þorw his lore shal leue Coueityse,
And be adradde of Deth and with-drawe hym fram Pryde,
And acorde with Conscience and kisse her either other.'   [970
    Thus thorw Hende-speche entred þe frere,
And cam in to Conscience and curteisly hym grette.
'Þow art welcome,' quod Conscience. 'Canstow hele þe syke?
Here is Contricioun,' quod Conscience, 'my cosyn, y-wounded;
Conforte hym,' quod Conscience, 'and take kepe to his sores.   [975
The plastres of þe persoun and poudres biten to sore,
He lat hem ligge ouerlonge and loth is to chaunge hem;
Fro Lenten to Lenten he lat his plastres bite.'
'That is ouerlonge,' quod this limitour, 'I leue I shal amende it';
And goth and gropeth Contricioun and gaf hym a plastre   [980
Of 'a pryue payement, and I shal praye for ȝow,
For alle that ȝe ben holde to al my lyf-tyme,
And make ȝow, my lady, in masse and in matynes,
As freres of owre fraternite, for a litel syluer'.

letters and obtained his written authority to hear confessions
in districts where he travelled. He came where Conscience
was, and knocked at the gate. Peace, the doorkeeper of Unity,
unlocked it and quickly asked him what he wanted.

'Truly,' said the friar, 'I desire to talk to Contrition, to
promote advantage and healing. That is why I have come
here.'

'He is ill,' said Peace, 'and so are many others. Hypocrisy
has wounded them; it is going to be very difficult for them to
recover.'

'I am a surgeon,' said the friar, 'and know how to make
healing ointments. Conscience is well acquainted with me
and with my abilities.'

Then Peace said: 'If you please, before you go any further,
what are you called? Do not conceal your name, I beg you!'

'Certainly', said his companion. 'I am Sir Creeper-into-
houses.'

'Take yourself off!' said Peace. 'By God! Unless you
possess some special skill, you are not coming in here, in
spite of all your medicines! Less than eight years ago, I once
knew a man like you, dressed in a cope in the same way, who
entered a court where I was living and became both my lord's
and my lady's doctor. Finally, when my lord was out, this
friar gave such treatment to our women that some of them
were with child.'

Courteous-Speech told Peace to open the gates. 'Let the
friar and his companion in and give them a good welcome!
It may be that he will use his eyes and ears to such effect that,
as a result of his teaching, Life will abandon Covetousness and
come to fear Death, sever himself from Pride and make his
peace with Conscience in a mutual embrace.'

So, thanks to Courteous-Speech, the friar gained entrance.
He made his way in to Conscience and greeted him cour-
teously.

'I am glad to see you', said Conscience. 'Can you heal the
sick? My cousin, Contrition, lies here wounded. Comfort
him, and attend to his sores! The parson's plasters and pow-
ders are too astringent. He keeps them on too long and is
reluctant to change them, leaving his plasters to smart from
one Lent to the next.'

'That is too long', said the friar. 'I think I can put it right.'

He went and prodded Contrition with his fingers and gave
him a plaster made of 'a confidential payment, and I will

L

Thus he goth and gadereth and gloseth þere he shryueth,   [985
Tyl Contricioun hadde clene forȝeten to crye and to wepe,
And wake for his wykked werkes, as he was wont to done.
For confort of his confessour, Contricioun he lafte,
Þat is þe souereynest salue for alkyn synnes.
   Sleuth seigh þat and so did Pryde,   [990
And come with a kene wille Conscience to assaille.
Conscience cryde eft and bad Clergye help hym,
And also Contricioun forto kepe þe ȝate.
'He lith and dremeth,' seyde Pees, 'and so do many other;
The frere with his phisik þis folke hath enchaunted,   [995
And plastred hem so esyly þei drede no synne.'
'Bi Cryste,' quod Conscience þo, 'I wil bicome a pilgryme,
And walken as wyde as al þe worlde lasteth,
To seke Piers þe Plowman, þat Pryde may destruye,
And þat freres hadde a fyndyng, þat for nede flateren,   [1000
And contrepleteth me, Conscience; now Kynde me auenge,
And sende me happe and hele til I haue Piers þe Plowman!'
And sitthe he gradde after grace til I gan awake.

---

⁹⁹⁸ worlde: MS wordle

pray for you and for all your close relations as long as I live. And you, my lady, I will make part of my intention at Mass and Mattins, as if you belonged to the brothers of our Order, in return for a little money.'

So he went about taking his pickings, and flattering when he heard confessions, until Contrition had clean forgotten to cry and weep and keep vigils for his evil deeds, as he used to do. His confessor comforted him so well that he abandoned contrition, which is the most sovereign remedy for every kind of sin. Sloth observed this, and so did Pride, and advanced with eager desire to attack Conscience. Conscience cried out again, bidding Learning to help him and Contrition to hold the gate.

'He lies dreaming,' said Peace, 'and so do many others. The friar has cast a spell over people with his medicines. The plasters he has given them are so easy to bear that they have no fear of any sins.'

Then Conscience said: 'By Christ! I will become a pilgrim and walk to the utmost ends of the earth to seek Piers the Ploughman, who can destroy Pride and provide an honest living for these friars who, out of necessity, become flatterers and oppose me, who am Conscience. Now may Nature avenge me, and prosper and heal me, until I find Piers the Ploughman!'

Then he cried out for grace, until I awoke.

Abbreviations

AV: The Authorised Version of the Bible.

BCP: The Book of Common Prayer.

Bennett: *Langland, Piers Plowman: the Prologue and Passus I-VII of the B text as found in Bodleian MS. Laud Misc. 581 , Edited with Notes and Glossary* by J. A. W. Bennett (Oxford, 1972).

Goodridge: *Langland, Piers the Plowman: a new translation* by J. F. Goodridge (Penguin Classics, 1959).

OED: Oxford English Dictionary.

Salter: *Piers Plowman*, edited by Elizabeth Salter and Derek Pearsall (*York Medieval Texts*, London, 1967).

Skeat: *The Vision of William concerning Piers the Plowman, in three parallel texts*, edited by W. W. Skeat, 2 vols (Oxford, 1886). References in the Notes to the complete text are to this edition.

Notes

A

(Prologue, lines 1-99)

2   Most editors have taken *shepe* to mean 'shepherd', but Bennett argues in favour of 'sheep', basing his argument on the spelling of the word. Neither translation gives completely satisfactory sense, but, on the whole, 'shepherd' seems to involve the less strained interpretation.

3   The point of the comparison is that a hermit who went wandering about the country would be 'unholy' because his rule of life demanded that he should remain within his cell.

44   Langland's *roberdes knaues* are the *Roberdesmen*, notorious bands of wandering lawbreakers, mentioned in fourteenth-century statutes as the perpetrators of 'divers manslaughters, felonies and robberies'.

62   *maistres* and *freris* are in apposition. The meaning is not 'principal' friars, but friars who are 'Masters' in the academic sense.

75   A ragman was a 'ragged' roll of parchment on which the answers to enquiries made by royal justices on their visitations up and down the country were inscribed. The bottom of the parchment was cut into strips, to which the seals of the witnesses were attached. The transferred use of the term here suggests the visual resemblance of the Pardoner's Bull of Indulgence, with its edge hung with episcopal seals, to such rolls. For a fuller account of the *ragman*, see Bennett, pp. 90 f.

86   The terse phrase 'sing for simony' is a topical allusion to the abuses made possible by the proliferation of chantry chapels, endowed by individuals or by guilds, in which masses for the souls of the founders were to be sung. The terms on which priests or clerks could obtain chantries might involve them in simony, the sin of Simon Magus to whom St Peter said: 'Your silver perish with you, because you thought you could obtain the gift of God with money!' (Acts VIII 20).

92   i.e. by taking office in the king's exchequer.

94   The translation is based on the suggestion made by Bennett (p. 94) that *wardes* and *wardmotes* refer to the two different senses that can be attached to the word 'ward': (1) a minor under guardship and (2) a division of a city.

(Prologue, lines 146-209)

144   There seems to be clear reference here to the situation that arose in England when the Black Prince died before his father, Edward III,

leaving the young child, the future Richard II, as heir to the throne. The 'cat' has generally been taken to represent Edward III, but Bennett suggests an equation with the Protector, John of Gaunt. The whole treatment of the fable of belling the cat hints at topical allusions—an impression confirmed by the Dreamer's declared unwillingness to interpret his dream.

160   An alternative interpretation of *coupled and uncoupled*—'jointly or severally'—is put forward by Bennett.

(Passus I, lines 1-207)

178   Literally, 'with skin and with face'.

204   This whole line is difficult—not only to the modern reader but, clearly, to the medieval reader, since the scribes of the various manuscripts of the poem have produced different versions. The version given here is composite, but seems to make the best sense. For a fuller note see Bennett, p. 106.

217   Literally, 'righteous reason'. *Reason*, in Middle English, has an extra dimension which has now been lost. It is not merely the faculty of intellectual knowledge, but also the faculty of moral knowledge, which distinguishes between the principles of good and evil.

240   Literally, 'brought me sureties to fulfil my commands'. One cannot render this condensed statement exactly in modern English; some expansion is necessary. Holy Church's argument refers to Baptism. She first 'received' the Dreamer in his baptism; his godparents were the 'sureties' who promised, on his behalf, to fulfil her commands. *Borwe*, in Middle English, has the sense both of a pledge and of someone who stands surety for a pledge. See *OED* s.v. *Borrow*, sb. 1 and 2.

244   *Kyndeli* really means 'naturally', but the force of 'naturally' has so greatly weakened in modern English that the word can no longer convey the sense of something deeply and intuitively felt, with the whole of one's physical and spiritual nature.

246   Literally 'this same thing'.

309   *Triacle*, which has become modern English *treacle*, has, as its ultimate source-sense, 'an antidote against a venomous bite' and is used in Middle English in the sense of a 'kind of salve . . . antidote against venomous bites, poisons generally, and malignant diseases'. See *OED* s.v. *treacle*, 1.

310   *Spise* may mean 'spice' or it may mean 'species'. The root lies in Latin *species*, but the word reached English via Old French, in which *species* has a double development: *espice* 'spice' and *espece* 'a kind, a species'. As a result, there is considerable confusion in Middle English, both in spelling and in meaning. In the present context, it may be taken either as 'that kind (of remedy for sin)' (Skeat), or as 'a figurative use of *spise*, i.e. the aromatic substance derived from plants' (Bennett).

313   *plente of pees*. Skeat and Bennett equate *plente* with *plante/plonte*, to accord with the readings of the A and C texts, but this is unnecessary

for an understanding of the B-text version. Langland has a complex image in mind in this passage: (i) the sheer weight of love, which sent it tumbling down from heaven to earth; (ii) the more fleeting suggestion of the leaf on a lime-tree branch. *Plente* 'plenty' allies itself with the weight of love; *plante* 'plant' allies itself with the leaf on the lime-tree. There is no reason why a poet, at different times of his life, should not prefer now one, now the other, possible stress on different aspects of his imagery, though, no doubt, his readers are intended to keep both aspects simultaneously in mind.

316   i.e. until Love, in the Person of Christ, became incarnate.

339   Langland's play on the now almost obsolete *mete*, 'meet, measure' and *mesures* can be seen also in the rendering of this text in the AV: 'With what measure ye mete, it shall be measured to you again'.

(Passus II, lines 1-236)

377   *Favel* is a proper name, taken from the Old French *Roman de Fauvel*, where it is used 'to name a personification of duplicity, fraud, or intrigue' (Bennett). *Flattery* is used here in translation because modern Englsih tends to run out of synonyms for the various shades of falsehood represented in this part of the poem.

385   Certain precious stones were traditionally credited with curative or preventive powers.

391   It is not easy to give an alternative name to Meed without begging the question of the precise significance which Langland attaches to her. She represents the *use* of worldly goods, rather than worldly goods themselves, and therefore includes the principle of fair payment on the one hand, and bribery on the other. Her equivocal nature accounts for her equivocal parentage. Her father is Falsehood, but her mother is *Amendes* —the making of restitution.

398   This may simply be a proverbial saying: 'Like father, like son', but the words are an exact quotation from the *Quicunque Vult* (the so-called Athanasian Creed), where the reference is to God the Father and God the Son. Since Langland is drawing a parallel between the lineage of Meed and the lineage of Holy Church, it is not unreasonable to suppose that he intends a deliberate, ironic reference. His familiarity with the *Quicunque Vult* is unquestionable, since he later uses it to provide the words of a pardon given to Piers the Ploughman.

437   *Beire wille*: 'the desire of them both'. *Beire* is a survival of the Old English inflected genitive plural.

445 ff.   Meed's wedding-charter is deliberately modelled on the form of legal charters. Not only the obviously 'learned' opening, *sciant presentes et futuri*, but the subsequent phrases *to haue and to holde*, *ʒeldyng for þis þinge*, *In þe date of . . .*, *Bi siʒte of . . .* all correspond to the formulae used to set out the various stages of a charter. Langland is not alone in using the charter-form as an allegorical device; it is also found in two other fourteenth-century texts, *The Charter of the Abbey of the Holy Ghost* and

the group of works collectively known as *The Middle English Charters of Christ*. There, however, the allegory is used for serious and devout purposes. Langland's combination of the device with the extra element of ironic parody seems to have no parallel in other Middle English writings.

478   It is not clear what is meant by *of Paulynes doctrine*. Skeat takes it to refer to the Order of Crutched Friars, or *Paulines*; Bennett points out that 'friars were not usually pardoners' and suggests that perhaps there is 'an allusion to St Paul's or its neighbourhood, the haunt of priests and clerks'. This interpretation is strengthened by the further reference to *Paulynes* in line 547, where the linking of them with the Consistory Courts suggests a London connection.

540   *Prouisoures*, here, are clergy presented 'with an ecclesiastical living by the pope, before the death of the actual incumbent' (Skeat). Such papal interference was a cause of great resentment and led to a statute designed to prevent it.

599   The exact statement of this curious length of time is probably a deliberate topical reference: 'Six months and eleven days was exactly the length of Edward III's French campaign, 1359-60' (Bennett).

B

(Passus V, lines 1-62)

11   To the modern reader, Reason may seem an odd choice of preacher. Once again (cf. note to A 217), one must remember that, in Middle English, *Reason* is the faculty of moral, as well as of intellectual, know-ledge. Consequently, Reason exercises many of the functions which we should now feel to belong to Conscience. Broadly speaking, Reason provides the principles of moral knowledge, Conscience acts upon them. Although here, as elsewhere in the poem, Reason seems to be considering particular cases, in fact he is arguing a single general moral theme, which might be summed up as: 'Fulfil the obligations of your own particular calling or state of life, whatever they may be'.

14   This is a reference to a particularly severe gale, well-attested in con-temporary records, which occurred on a Saturday during the winter of 1361-2.

26   *Purfyle* is the embroidered or furred trimming of a dress.

32   Skeat suggests that the unusual masculine name *Bette* is the equivalent of *Bat*, i.e. Bartholomew.

50   The meaning of *if tresoun ne were* is not certain. Possibly one can take it as: 'if it were not for treason'—that is, the people are the king's 'treasure' unless treason spoils the relationship. Bennett tentatively suggests that the implication may be: 'though there is no defence against treason'. The first of these interpretations is used in the translation.

52   It is tempting to see *grace* as a special papal Indulgence, but Bennett points out that this 'specific sense . . . does not seem to be evidenced in

English'. Whatever interpretation one gives, *grace*, here, clearly comes under the second main category of meanings given by *OED*, namely, *favour*. The general meaning seems to be that the pope should first be quite sure of the righteousness of his own actions; only then can he properly extend 'favour' or 'mercy' or 'forgiveness' to others.

59   *Qui cum patre et filio.* This is a telescoped allusion to the traditional close of liturgical prayers, technically known as the Ascription of Glory to the Godhead. The formula is flexible. Its precise wording depends on which particular Person of the Trinity has primarily been invoked. Since Langland here uses the form: 'who with the Father and the Son', he obviously regards the Holy Ghost as having been already mentioned. The *seynt Treuthe* of the preceding line must, therefore, be seen as a reference to the Holy Ghost.

62   *Wille* may be a proper name or it may be a passing personification of the faculty of the human will. Since, at a later point in the poem, the Dreamer says: 'My name is Longe Wille', it is tempting to assume that *Wille*, here, represents the personal name and that the Dreamer is identifying himself with all those who are moved to repentance by Reason's sermon. There can, however, be no certainty.

(Passus V, lines 134–303)

97   If a prioress were a priest, she would have the right to hear confessions. The implied argument is this: what is heard in confession must remain inviolably secret; women are incapable of keeping secrets; therefore, if a prioress were allowed to hear confessions, she would immediately break this fundamental rule.

136   Literally, 'if the grace of guile had not gone in amongst my goods'. The translation is deliberately free, in order to bring out the parody of 'the grace of God' contained in the phrase *þe grace of gyle*.

138   The *donet* took its name from the work of a fourth-century grammarian, Donatus. In the course of the Middle Ages it came to represent a primary textbook.

147   The lively, though involved, description of methods of commercial trickery can be summed up as the use of false weights and measures. If cloth is purchased by the yard, unfair stretching on the part of the vendor can make the number of yards seem greater than it really is. If spinners are given wool to make up into cloth and are paid according to the weight of the finished material, they can be cheated if the amount of wool originally handed out to them is weighed on a balance which registers more than the correct weight.

154   This clearly suggests the still familiar trick of charging an exorbitant price for liquor bought 'by the glass' when the 'glass' is an uncertain measure, readily lending itself to various forms of cheating.

155   Although *regratere* and the associated abstract noun *regraterye* refer to a retailer's dealings with the public, they are far from neutral words. They imply 'profiteering, including participation in combinations or price

rings' (Bennett). Skeat connects *hokkerye* with *hawker*—'door-to-door salesman'. Again, the phrase has a modern ring; the doorstep hawker still tends to ask far too much for his goods.

173   The 'cross' referred to here is the cross imprinted on the reverse of coins, not Christ's Cross.

178   One cannot be certain of the exact meaning of *eschaunges*, but it is probably a euphemism for dubious monetary transactions.

181   The *taille* is a 'tally-stick', a rough and ready method of accounting. A stick was marked with notches, which showed the amount of money received in payment of a debt. The stick was then split. Both the creditor and the debtor retained a split half; by the evidence of the notches, debt and payment could be balanced against each other.

184   This particular aspect of Avarice's knavery has to be taken in connection with the preceding lines. To conceal obvious usury, a loan could take the form of goods, *chaffare* (line 176), which would then be repurchased by the lender at a low valuation. The implication here is that lords and knights 'had to forfeit silks and cloths rightfully theirs or sell back at a cheap rate those bought by the feigned sale alluded to above' (Bennett). Skeat says that Avarice 'ironically calls his customers mercers and drapers'; the irony may well be deeper and more bitter than the modern reader realises. Langland has a strong feeling for the exercise of behaviour properly fitting to one's calling or state in life, and it seems likely that he intends here a profound condemnation of Avarice's action in causing knights to behave like tradesmen.

(Passus V, lines 485-651)

243   The idea of Christ's taking on man's nature like a garment can be traced back to liturgical sources. An effective use of it can be seen in a fourteenth-century lyric by William Herebert, which contains the line: 'My robe he hath upon'. Langland picks up the image again, in a more specific form, in his account of the Passion (see Section D), where he represents Christ as fighting in the armour of Piers the Ploughman, which is human nature.

245   This is the reading of the AV and BCP. The Common Bible reading does not exactly correspond.

248   No really satisfactory explanation of the phrase *mele tyme of seintes* has been found. Probably it represents a condensed running-together of several ideas and allusions: (i) the noon-time beginning of the Crucifixion; (ii) the redemption of the *seintes*—the souls of the righteous who awaited Christ's coming—initiated at that moment; (iii) the transference of Christ's offering of His human body on the Cross into the consecration of the bread and wine in the Eucharist, by which the faithful are fed by His body and blood; (iv) such traditional images as 'bread of angels', applied to Christ.

284   Pilgrims collected tokens of the particular shrines which they had visited, much as modern secular travellers collect badges. Details con-

cerning pilgrims' tokens can be found in the notes of Skeat, Goodridge, Bennett and Salter.

313   *St Thomas's shrine*: i.e. the much revered shrine of St Thomas Becket at Canterbury.

342   *Wit* and *Will* are seen as opposing forces in English texts from the beginning of the thirteenth century onwards. Both words have complex connotations, but when, as here, they are set in straight contrast, the rough distinction is between reason, on the one hand, and the ungoverned reliance on the senses and the emotions on the other.

346   Here again, there seems to be an allusion to the words of the *Quicunque vult*: 'This is the Catholick Faith: which except a man believe faithfully, he cannot be saved'.

361   The exact reference of *he* is not clear. The simplest interpretation seems to be to take it as a masculine pronoun, referring back to the personification of Amendment. This is the sense used here in translation. Bennett's suggestion that the reference could be to ' "Treuthe"—God the Father' raises problems about the mention of 'the king'. It is just possible that *he* should be taken as a feminine pronoun, deriving from the Old English *heo*, 'she'. In that case, the holder of 'the key of the latch' would be the Blessed Virgin Mary. The reading of the C-text of the poem clearly supports this interpretation. Possibly here, as occasionally elsewhere, Langland is struggling, in the course of his revisions, from a cloudy to a precise idea.

375   The nature of the Seven Deadly Sins has long been firmly established. The nature of the Seven Virtues has never been quite so clear. Perhaps the formulation of them was prompted, in the first place, by the medieval love of numerical correspondences. They can be seen as comprising the three 'theological' virtues of Faith, Hope and Charity and the four 'cardinal' virtues of Temperance, Fortitude, Prudence and Justice (or Righteousness). Alternatively, they can be seen as the direct antitheses of the sins of Pride, Avarice, Envy, Anger, Lechery, Gluttony and Sloth. The 'seven sisters' here represent the antithetical virtues, though not in a strictly exact form.

C

(Passus XIII, lines 21-147)

3   The meaning of *clergy* has narrowed over the centuries. In Middle English, it includes the modern sense of 'those in Holy Orders', but it also means 'learned men' or when, as used here, as an abstract noun, 'learning, literacy'. The connection of ideas seems clear since, for so long, only 'the clergy' were 'learned'.

6   *Scripture*, like *clergy*, can bear a wider sense in Middle English than that now current. Langland generally uses the word to refer simply to the Bible, but he can extend the reference to include other works regarded as possessing authority.

49   *Periculum est in falsis fratribus*. The point lies in the double application of
      fratres: 'brothers' in the general sense and 'friars' (i.e. the Brothers
      belonging to a religious Order) in the special sense.

63   Possibly the full sting of the insult of *Iurdan* 'jordan', 'chamber-pot',
      lies in a punning reference to a contemporary friar. Fr A. Gwynn ('The
      Date of the B-Text of *Piers Plowman*', *Review of English Studies* XIX,
      1943, pp. 1 ff.) draws attention to Miss M. E. Marcett's identification of
      Langland's gluttonous friar with a 'William Jordan, a restless Dominican
      controversialist of these years'. Skeat shows that *Iust* 'is not to be ex-
      plained as *just* . . . but is the word *juste*, in its signification of flagon,
      bottle or wine-jar'.

70   The friars' *Pocalips* is the medieval Latin *Apocalipsis Goliae*, often
      ascribed to Walter Mapes, a parody of the Biblical *Apocalypse*, in which
      a description of gluttonous monks is to be found. The identity of *seynt
      Auereys* is mysterious. The most promising identification seems to be that
      given by Skeat, who identifies her with 'St Avoya, who was fed with
      delicately white and sweet bread from heaven'.

73   The meaning of the phrase *testifye of a trinitee* is obscure. Goodridge
      takes it to signify: 'preach to you about trinities', a forceful but free
      translation. On the whole, it seems justifiable to adopt, in translation, the
      reading of the C-text revision: *take witnesse of the trinite*. The only really
      significant difference between B and C is the substitution of *the* for *a*;
      testifye and *take witnesse* seem to mean much the same thing, and *of*—a
      preposition capable of bearing supple variations of meaning—can well
      bear an identical meaning in both texts.

74   *Freyel* 'basket' survives in the modern English dialectal *frail*, 'a soft
      flexible basket, made of rushes or grass' (*English Dialect Dictionary* s.v.
      frail, sb. 1).

89   The *ȝonge childern* are presumably those who were made members of the
      Order at an early age—'novice-boys', as Goodridge calls them. Skeat
      hints that 'strange rumours were afloat as to the treatment of sick friars
      by their companions'.

99   The *seuene sones* of Learning are the traditional Seven Arts, or Seven
      Sciences. Grammar, logic and rhetoric were the substance of the
      trivium, the first part of a scholar's education; music, arithmetic, geometry
      and astronomy made up the *quadrivium*—further education.

107 f. A convincing and illuminating interpretation of these puzzling lines has
      been provided by Miss P. M. Kean ('Justice, Kingship and the Good Life
      in the second part of *Piers Plowman*', *Piers Plowman, Critical Approaches*,
      ed. S. S. Hussey, London, 1969, p. 92). She suggests that the use of
      infinites here reflects the specialised use of *infinitus* by medieval scholastic
      logicians to refer to negative concepts, 'indefinites' in the way that the
      word is used, for example, in speaking of an 'indefinite noun'. Her
      comment, on which the present translation is based, runs: 'Dowel and
      Dobet, then, are indefinites until, through the working of faith, they
      find definition in Dobest, that is, achieve their object and, instead of
      undefined possibility, gain actual realization'.

(Passus XIII, lines 172-460; Passus XIV, lines 1-52)

140   In asking Conscience whether he wishes to solve riddles, Learning is harking back to a passage not included here—a mysterious riddling charm-formula with which Patience concludes his speech (lines 115-127). Within this riddle-charm, he says, Dowel is bound. For a full discussion of the riddle see Goodridge, pp. 299 ff.

180   The distinction between Active Life and Contemplative Life is often made in medieval writings. T. P. Dunning has pointed out that the distinction is not always necessarily between two separate modes of living: 'unless the writer is expressly referring to the religious *state*, he uses the terms "active" and "contemplative" to denote two forms of activity of the *one* person, two aspects of the spiritual life of every man' ('Action and contemplation in *Piers Plowman*', *Piers Plowman, Critical Approaches*, p. 215).

280   *Et alibi: filij hominum* . . . The translation of Psalm LVII, verse 4, used here is that of the AV, which is closer to the Vulgate reading than that of the Common Bible.

(Passus XV, lines 1-39)

429   The phrase *make mone* is not an accurate representation of the Latin quotation from St Isidore on which Langland bases this passage. The Latin *recolit* means 'remembered', not 'complained'.

(Passus XV, lines 145-262)

443 ff. English is at a disadvantage in rendering the *c(h)aritas* of the Vulgate. From the early sixteenth century onwards, there has been dispute as to whether the appropriate biblical texts, particularly the thirteenth chapter of I Corinthians, should speak of *love* or of *charity*. *Charity* is adopted in translation here, to fit in with Langland's phraseology, but the full sense of *love* must be applied if one is to understand the proper meaning of the passage.

461   According to Skeat, '*Tarse* was the name of a kind of silken stuff . . . said to have come from a country called *Tharsia* adjoining Cathay (China)'.

504   *Petrus, id est Christus* is a baffling and much discussed phrase. The genesis of the half-line is perfectly clear; it depends on the conflation of two biblical texts: 'You are Peter, and on this rock I will build my church' (Matthew XVI 18) and 'they drank from the supernatural Rock which followed them, and the Rock was Christ' (I Corinthians X 4). The full point is inevitably lost in any English biblical translation. One needs to return to the Vulgate and the Latin play on *Petrus* (Peter) and *petra* (rock): 'tu es Petrus, et super hanc petram aedificabo ecclesiam meam'. *Petra*, again, is the word used for 'the Rock' who 'was Christ'. In the end, a logical explanation of the half-line is probably not possible. The simplest way seems to be to regard it as a highly complex poetic running together of associations: Piers, St Peter (and possibly his successors, the popes), the rock which provides the sure foundation of the Church, the rock which is Christ.

521 *Ycalled*, as Skeat points out, is to be connected with 'caul'—i.e. 'wearing a cap'. He connects *ycrimiled* with Old French *cresmeler* 'to anoint with holy oil'. Goodridge prefers to see *ycrimiled* as meaning 'a fringe of crimped hair'—'the waved hair on that part of the head which was left unshorn' by the tonsure.

D

(Passus XVIII, lines 1-431)

8 The source of the line lies in the Palm Sunday processional hymn, 'Gloria, laus et honor tibi sit, rex Christe, redemptor . . .', familiar in the English version:

> All glory, laud, and honour
> To thee, Redeemer, King,
> To whom the lips of children
> Made sweet Hosannas ring.

Gerlis, modern English 'girls', applied in Langland's day to children of either sex.

9 Skeat clearly regards *by orgonye* as meaning 'singing to an organ or other instrumental accompaniment'. Such an interpretation is quite possible, but, since Langland is here thinking of the spontaneous singing in the streets of Jerusalem on the first Palm Sunday, the likelier explanation is that he has in mind the medieval form of singing and writing for voices known as *organum*. The precise nature of *organum* is highly technical; for details see Dom Anselm Hughes, *The New Oxford History of Music II*; *Early Medieval Music up to 1300* (London, 1954) and Gustave Rees, *Music in the Middle Ages* (London, 1941). Very roughly speaking, *organum* involved the interplay of voices of different pitch, with the tenor holding the melody proper while the upper voice or voices engaged in elaborate, extended descant.

15 In a passage not included here, leading up to the account of Palm Sunday and the Passion, Langland identifies Faith with Abraham. This identification throws light on the presentation of Faith in this line and on the reference to *Olde Iuwes of Ierusalem*.

22 The image of Christ as a knight 'jousting' for man's redemption is not peculiar to Langland; it can also be seen, for example, in some of the religious lyrics. Langland's coupling of the image with the idea of Christ's 'jousting' in Piers's 'armour' of 'human nature' to conceal His divine nature reduces to a brief poetic allusion the knotty theological subtleties involved in attempts to define the dual nature of Christ.

35 The reference is to the Vulgate reading of Hosea XIII 14, here translated literally.

108 This is not an exact quotation, but a free summary of the ideas expressed in Daniel IX 24-26.

109   *Her kyngdom* literally means 'their kingdom'. In turning a narrative into direct speech, there has been a momentary confusion of personal possessive pronouns.

111 f. Though other sources are suggested by Skeat and Goodridge, the simplest explanation of the two Latin phrases seems to be to take them as allusions to the Apostles' Creed and the Nicene Creed respectively, given in this translation in the wording of the BCP.

115 ff. The whole episode is Langland's version of the widespread medieval allegory, occurring in various forms, commonly known as 'the four Daughters of God', which developed from the text: 'Mercy and truth are met together: righteousness and peace have kissed each other' (Psalm LXXXV 10, AV and BCP, LXXXIV, Vulagte). See Introduction.

160   *Ars vt artem falleret* is a clear allusion, though not precisely quoted, to the Passion hymn *Pange, lingua*, . . . 'Sing, my tongue, the glorious battle . . .', where it is suggested that the 'art' of man's destroyer must be matched by 'art'. The same source seems to underlie Christ's words *go gyle aʒeine gyle!* in line 355. *Þat was tynt þorw tre tree shal it wynne* (line 140) also reflects the phraseology of *Pange, lingua*.

163   Behind *Riʒtwisnesse* 'Rightousness' lies the Latin *Justitia* 'Justice'. This colours the nature of the arguments used by Righteousness.

218 f. The syntax of these two lines is not entirely clear. An alternative translation would be: 'And later permitted him to sin and to feel sorrow, in order to learn what happiness is and to know it with all his being'.

248   A reference to a detail in the apocryphal Gospel of Nicodemus, the early source from which the extended accounts of the Harrowing of Hell derive.

250   No clear meaning can be attached to the phrase '*Gygas* the geaunt . . .'. The C-text reads 'Iesus as a gyaunt', which makes much better sense. The 'giant-like' Samson, breaking down the gates of Gaza, was an accepted type—that is, an Old Testament foreshadowing—of Christ breaking the gates of hell.

335   Skeat points out that 'the serpent who tempted Eve was sometimes represented with short feet, like a lizard or crocodile, and the face of a young maiden'.

377 ff. The point of this comment is brought out by Skeat, who quotes cases of a hanged man reviving after his apparent death, particularly a case in Leicester in 1363, when Edward III saw the cart pass in which the seeming corpse was being taken to burial, and gave the man his charter of pardon.

380   The rather imprecise phrase *or otherwise* might suggest that there is a question whether the man should be put to death or not, but the C-text reading *other Iuwise*, where *Iuwise*, derived from Old French *juise*, means 'judgment, sentence of death', supports an interpretation which leaves the man's intended punishment in no doubt.

421   The translation of the Psalm text is taken from the AV and BCP, since the wording of the Common Bible is not so directly relevant to the participants in the allegorical encounter.

(Passus XIX, lines 1-64)

442   The statement *Or it is Pieres þe Plowman* is changed in the C-text to question form: *Or is it . . .?* This clearly improves the sense. However, the statement-form for a question can also be seen in D 186: 'or þow art riȝt dronke'.

458   The interpretation of Christ as 'conqueror' may result from a mis-understanding of the etymology of *Christ*, 'the Anointed', or from an extension of the idea of 'the Lord's Anointed'. For the differing views see Skeat and Goodridge respectively.

(Passus XIX, lines 194-443)

543   Skeat suggests that *Foluyles lawes* are 'laws of the character of Lynch laws, and were (similarly) so named from some now forgotten worthy'.

577   'The operation really intended is that the cook shall watch over the pot, and gently stir it when it seems likely to boil over' (Skeat).

585   Skeat explains that *maister Iohan* is 'merely a contemptuous name for a cook'.

(Passus XX, lines 50-384)

862 f.   The play on *good hope* and *wanhope* 'despair' is no doubt deliberate. Goodridge's expanded translation: 'Old Age seized the sword of Good Hope' is attractive, but one cannot be certain that Langland intends *hent* to be taken quite so literally in the sense of physical seizing.

866   By the 'glass cap' Langland means that a purely illusory protection against sickness was offered.

909   The 'giants' are the Seven Deadly Sins.